LIVING ISLAM OUT LOUD

LIVING ISLAM OUT LOUD

American Muslim Women Speak

Edited by Saleemah Abdul-Ghafur

BEACON PRESS, BOSTON

BEACON PRESS

25 Beacon Street
Boston, Massachusetts 02108-2892
www.beacon.org

Beacon Press books
are published under the auspices of
the Unitarian Universalist Association of Congregations.

08 07 06 05   8 7 6 5 4 3 2 1

This book is printed on acid-free paper that meets the uncoated
paper ANSI/NISO specifications for permanence as revised in 1992.

Text design by Patricia Duque Campos
Composition by Wilsted & Taylor Publishing Services

Library of Congress Cataloging-in-Publication Data

Living Islam out loud : American Muslim women speak /
edited by Saleemah Abdul-Ghafur.— 1st ed.
p.   cm.
ISBN 0-8070-8383-6 (pbk. : alk. paper)
1. Muslim women—United States—Biography. 2. Muslim women—
Religious life—United States. 3. Women in Islam—United States.
I. Abdul-Ghafur, Saleemah.

BP67.A1L58 2005
297'.082'0973—dc22   2004028161

In Memory of
Sharifa Al Khateeb

For
Kaylah and Kai

CONTENTS

This anthology is about women who don't remember a time when they weren't both American and Muslim. We are the children of immigrants from Pakistan, Egypt, and Senegal. We are the distant descendants of African slaves brought to the Americas as well as the children of American men and women who accepted Islam in adulthood. Unlike us, our parents were raised largely in other countries or in other faith traditions. Our education was a colorful mix of home schooling, the local mosque, and Public School #9. We wore Underoos and watched MTV. We know *juz 'amma* (the final thirtieth of the Qur'an) and Michael Jackson's *Thriller* by heart. We played Atari and Game Boy and competed in Qur'anic recitation competitions. As we enter our twenties, thirties, and forties we have settled into the American Muslim identity that we've pioneered.

Some of us were told that there was no need to craft an American Muslim identity—that we could simply apply the Qur'an and the *sunnah* (traditions of the Prophet Muhammad) to our lives. That is simplistic and unrealistic. For example, I do not observe the rules of *mahram* (requiring a lone female to travel with a male guardian). Nor can I imagine marrying the way the contemporaries of the Prophet Muhammad married (many women during the time of the Prophet married for political and business reasons, with none of the modern notions of love and marriage). In addition, much of the Islam we American Muslim women know was defined and interpreted abroad, in the larger Muslim world. It is Islam fused with foreign culture. That's why Muslim women in Senegal dress differently from Muslim women in Morocco—each culture has its own interpretation, and we in the United States are creating a distinctly American Muslim culture. American Muslim women are choosing a path that honors our Islamic faith and our American heritage without apology.

The paradox of September 11, 2001, is that it firmly and forever established Islam and Muslims in the eyes of the West. Muslims have been in the West for centuries, and in ever-increasing numbers since the mid-twentieth century, but the tragic events of 9/11 created an unparalleled awareness of our presence. The result is that Islam has gone mainstream, and it is suddenly clear just how profoundly ignorant Americans have been about Islam and Muslims. "Go home . . . back where you came from!" passersby yelled at my friends. I laughed when I heard these stories, because I thought, "Just where would that be?" My family has been in the United States for centuries. My parents accepted Islam in their twenties and I was raised as a Muslim in northern New Jersey. Home for me is New Jersey and I have never felt as though I wasn't American. At the same time, I was saddened because I understood that for many Americans, Islam and Muslims had an alien face—a face that resided outside of the "normative" human family and relegated us to perpetual "otherness."

While there are 1.2 billion Muslims worldwide, U.S. Census data and a recent study by Cornell University place the American Muslim population at around 7 million. Islam is the fastest growing religion in the world, and in the United States, the American Muslim population has exploded almost overnight. In the United States, Muslims are fairly spread out, with major cities hosting the highest concentration. The American Muslim population encompasses eighty different nationalities, with African Americans being the largest single ethnic group; of the remainder, about a third are of South Asian descent and another third of Middle Eastern or North African descent. American Muslims range in the way we practice Islam and in our affiliation with any particular Muslim community. I have yet to find data detailing the exact number of American Muslim women; that said, what is significant about the American Muslim population is that the data demonstrate that American Muslims are younger, more educated, and more affluent than the average American.

There are many misconceptions about Islam and Muslims, including the notion that all Muslims are recent immigrants and that all African American Muslims are from the Nation of Islam or became Muslim in prison. Various interpretations of the role of Muslim women in sacred Islamic texts and in contemporary society give rise to the biggest misconceptions of all—that we are oppressed, relegated to secondary status, and often placed on a pedestal similar to the suppressed women of the Victorian era. Very rarely do we encounter empowering images of American Muslim women.

The truth is that some Muslim women, both in the United States and abroad, are in fact oppressed in many ways and do not live self-determined lives. The truth is also that many Muslim women live powerful lives sourced from the freedom granted to us by God. No longer can mainstream institutions and individuals continue to paint Islam with the broad brush of rigidity, chauvinism, and antiquated notions. At the same time, more Muslims are acknowledging what ails our communities so that we can step into an egalitarian and humanistic future. God speaks to us in the Qur'an saying that He will not change our condition until we change what is in our hearts and souls.

I believe that Islam is in the midst of global transformation. This transformation is being led largely by Muslims in the West because we have certain academic freedoms along with freedom of speech and freedom to worship. These civil liberties are largely unknown in Muslim-majority countries. Those of us leading this transformation are confident in claiming Islam for ourselves. We recognize the problems within the Muslim community even as we critique the mainstream's rush to stereotype us. Now more than ever, the world needs to hear our voices.

Most of the books written about Islam and Muslims that are widely accessible to the mainstream are by people of other faith traditions. And many of the books written by American Muslims are about immigrants coping with assimilation, or else they offer conversion stories about why the grass is greener on the Muslim side. This book is about the first true generation of American Muslim women. That is, for the first time in history we have a critical mass of women under forty years old, raised as Muslims in the United States by parents who themselves struggled to reconcile their American and Muslim identities. We have never lived without Islam, nor did we grow up in Muslim-majority countries.

Over the past three years, I traveled around the nation and listened to the issues facing American Muslim women, which I have grouped as follows: intersecting identities, hijab, relationships, culture juxtaposed to Islam, sex and sexuality, activism, and spirituality. The essays in this anthology examine these issues through first-person accounts. Though it was not part of the plan, each contributor ended up discussing two of these issues no matter what else her piece was about: the juxtaposition of culture and Islam in general, and the question of hijab in particular. All of us have inherited cultural norms, which are embedded in our practice of Islam; no place is this more evident than in America, where there are so many ethnicities and nationalities represented among Muslims. Each culture comes with its own interpretation and manifestation of Islam. Similarly, each of the essays in this collection has a thread describing how ethnic culture is manifested in each author's practice of Islam and how our ethnic identity can supersede spirituality. In addition, each of us is individually creating an American Muslim identity, which in the aggregate form the beginnings of American Muslim culture.

Hijab is the other topic woven throughout these contributions. "Hijab" comes from an Arabic verb meaning "to veil, cover, screen, shelter, and/or seclude." In contemporary society it refers to the fabric some Muslim women use to cover their hair. For some it is a symbol of piety and modesty; for others it is a symbol of oppression and restriction. The Qur'an enjoins modesty in dress, speech, and actions for Islam's male and female adherents.

The topic of hijab has divided the Muslim community and is a lightning rod for debate and discussion—whether or not to do it and why, and what priority the topic should have among the issues facing Muslims.

There are many reasons a woman decides to wear hijab. Depending on whom you ask, some wear it because they believe it is mandated by God, others to demonstrate solidarity or resistance, and still others to follow familial and community mores. Conversely, there are many reasons a woman does not wear hijab. Some don't because they don't want to distinguish themselves in Western society; others don't believe that Islam requires hijab of its female followers, believing that modesty is required of all Muslims and in the broader sense regarding speech and actions as well as dress. Through our own personal narratives we reveal how we arrived at our choices about hijab. As you'll read, most of us are exhausted with the hijab debate and envision a future where we move beyond the judgments of women with and sans hijab.

The remaining topics—intersecting identities, relationships, sex and sexuality, activism, and spirituality—are discussed in specific chapters of the book. I am presenting my story first to frame this anthology and describe the experiences that shaped my life.

I chose the contributors to this anthology based on the following criteria: first, she must have been raised as a Muslim in America; second, she must be contributing to public life in an extraordinary way; and third, she must possess the will and courage to share honestly the experiences that shaped her life. Each of us is revealing parts of our lives—our challenges, triumphs, and innermost secrets—which, in many cases, neither our friends nor families know. And we have a great deal at stake. We risk judgment from our families, friends, the Muslim community, and the world. But we do it with the hope of creating a better future and because we know it's time for the world to hear our unfiltered voices.

We are Muslim women who have cleared our own paths and created ourselves both because and in spite of Islam and other

Muslims. Our American Muslim identity is not linear, nor can it be shed or separated. It just is. We are women who understand that following disempowering interpretations of sacred text isn't for us. We reflect the continuum of American Muslim women—some of us are still conflicted, while others are more secure with the choices we've made, but all of us are evolving as spiritual beings. Our group includes professionals and homemakers, Sunni and Shi'a, Democrats, Republicans, and independents. We hail from a variety of ethnic backgrounds, and while we disagree on many counts, we agree on the need for our voices to be heard and on our sisterhood. This book reflects the diversity of American Muslim women in all our complexity.

My overall intention for this book is to humanize American Muslim women to our fellow citizens of the world. For Muslim readers in particular, my intention is twofold. First, I hope that in hearing our stories, the masses of women who fear judgment and condemnation will find permission to claim their own experiences and a self-determined future. Finally, I pray that Muslim girls here and abroad will read these stories and avoid the missteps we've made, know acceptance and solidarity, and be ultimately inspired to live Islam out loud.

I was born Nefertiti Omowale Daniels on April 6, 1974. My parents became Muslim in their early twenties after searching for greater meaning in their lives. They had visited mosques and met Muslims and liked what they saw. Shortly after my birth they changed our names legally, and I became Saleemah Abdul-Ghafur. Saleemah means "peaceful" and Abdul means "servant of." Ghafur, one of God's attributes, means "the most forgiving." Growing up, I always remembered that I was the peaceful one who was a servant of God, the most forgiving.

I grew up in a middle-class suburb in New Jersey and had a fairly happy and sheltered childhood. My parents were fiercely overprotective, though they worked hard to ensure that I received the best education our community had to offer. Even though I had access to the best of Western education, I was isolated socially, and coed activities were completely out of the question. I had a small circle of friends of whom my parents approved. When it was time to go to college, my parents refused to allow me to live on campus. They believed campus life was antithetical to raising a good Muslim woman. I remember how sad I was during high school graduation because my entire senior class marched off to college campuses across the nation while I stayed home and commuted to college. Though I'd worn hijab off and on over the years, when I started college, my mother declared that it was time for me to wear hijab permanently, and so I marched off to the train wearing hijab.

My mother made all of the decisions about my life, and my father allowed her to, rarely intervening. He was old-school in the sense that he believed she knew the best way to raise a daughter. I was not rebellious and largely obeyed my parents, not wanting to displease them, so I became silent, repressing the sadness and anger I felt during those years. As a result of my upbringing, I never learned how to interact with men in a social and platonic way, since males who were not family members were strictly off limits. I always felt uncomfortable when a man approached me or spoke to me. I became defensive around men and internalized a general distrust of men.

The reason my mother gave for limiting my social sphere was simply "Muslims don't do that." And so I believed that these limitations were prescribed by Islam, and as a good Muslim girl, I should comply. The reward would be a picture-perfect life, which meant good grades, getting into a great college, marrying a wonderful man, having a baby within two years, and then, pursuing graduate school. I lived that illusion for many years.

In 1998 my parents and I went on hajj, the pilgrimage to Mecca. I turned twenty-four, praying with my family on the Mountain of Mercy in Arafat, Saudi Arabia. Our hajj was extraordinary. It opened my eyes to the universality of Islam and to the vast continuum of Muslims. We were millions—from every corner of the world, nomad and city dweller, old and young, rich and poor, united for this sacred spiritual journey; yet each of us stood alone before God, cleansing our souls and remembering our Abrahamic ancestors through rituals. I returned to the United States buoyant and renewed. And within six months, I'd received everything I prayed for on hajj, including a husband.

I met him in July, he proposed in October, and we were married in January. He was an American-born convert to Islam. He was handsome, charismatic, and matched my enthusiasm for adventure. He loved my outgoing, assertive personality and valued my accomplishments and ambitions. My family and friends embraced him easily and wholeheartedly. When we were married, I was a virgin; I had a bright career and grand notions of fulfilling my dreams. I was also as naive as a young bride could be. I believed I was a good catch and that we would enjoy a happy marriage because I had been a good Muslim girl. Many people in my community were anxiously awaiting my nuptials and turned out to witness the event. We had a huge wedding with all the stress and joy these milestones bring, and at the last moment, the *New York Times* asked to cover my wedding. They were interested in covering a Muslim wedding, and it certainly added some spice to the Sunday wedding section.

A few days into the honeymoon, on a cruise ship in the middle of the Caribbean, my husband stopped speaking to me. Shocked at the silent treatment, I coaxed the reason out of him, and he admitted frankly, "I don't want my wife to run the dinner conversation." My offense had been leading a discussion during our evening meal with our dinner partners. We talked it through but nothing was ever resolved. I thought this was just a bump along the way and that overall we'd be fine.

We returned home and the next few months demonstrated that I was not his idea of a proper Muslim wife. Somehow, I was always doing something inappropriate. Apparently, I even needed a lot of instruction on the correct way to do laundry and cut potatoes. We began to argue more frequently, and he would say that I didn't know how to be a woman. Days would go by and he would refuse to speak to me or to acknowledge my presence. He would come in at night and sleep on the other side of the bed, making no body contact, and in the morning he would leave without a word. This silent treatment was torture for me, so I would plead with him to speak to me or touch me, and occasionally his response was some reference from the Qur'an or a hadith. One time he justified the silence by quoting a hadith saying a Muslim could be angry with another Muslim for up to three days. When he was ready to make up, we would, and that would be followed by a period of harmony. I remember him kissing me one day as a reward, saying, "You've been really good lately." The peace never lasted, and the marriage became a regular assault on my sensibilities, which screamed at me to fight back and to leave, but I ignored my intuition for fear of the consequences.

Few people outside of our immediate circle knew of our troubles because in public we seemed to lead a content and happy life. Privately, I often sought advice from our parents, family members, and imams, which usually enraged my husband even more. We went through counseling with our family and with two imams. Though my parents were wary and increasingly alarmed at the stories of what was transpiring in my marriage, the imams attributed our problems to first-year newlywed adjustments. Finally, one imam agreed that a professional marriage counselor would be advisable. After a few sessions my husband refused to continue, remarking that I was the one with the problem who needed to go to counseling.

Over this time our arguments had worsened, and soon he became violent. First there was a push, then he slapped the phone from my hand, and finally one morning, after I woke him for prayer, he hit me in the face and threw me across the room. As I looked at my face, bloody and swollen in the bathroom mirror, my instinct said *call the police,* but I called my parents instead. While I waited for them to arrive, my husband paced through our apartment. He told me to wash my face and sat down to watch the morning news. My father arrived and took me home. I went to work, attending a full day of meetings, not explaining my swollen face and covering my bruises.

Over the next few days I stayed with my parents, and I learned that my husband had confessed what happened to an imam. The imam was upset and began a series of conversations with my husband and me. The imam was distressed because he had been one of the people who had endorsed my husband's character before our wedding, and now he felt a degree of responsibility. He noted that it is forbidden in Islam to hit someone in the face and instructed my husband to apologize immediately. He apologized to me, saying he didn't know that he couldn't hit someone in the face. Though I was outraged at the clinical nature of this discussion and the fact that anyone would need sacred text to know that physical abuse was unacceptable, I did not voice my outrage. The voice within me marked how ridiculous and dehumanizing this marriage had become. It whispered that I was committing myself to someone who had violated every boundary I'd ever established for myself. Even so, I returned to our apartment against my parents' wishes and my own better judgment.

That evening my husband apologized again and asked if I would forgive him. I replied "yes" and began to sob. My husband hugged me while I cried. I was crying because I wasn't strong enough to leave. I was crying because I was staying, knowing it wouldn't work out. I continued to cry, and his hugs turned to kisses and then to sex. I remember not wanting to have sex and lying there wanting to ask him never to hit me again, but again I was silent. In the back of my mind ran the hadith that I had heard during many Muslim wedding ceremonies. This hadith stated that if a man approached his wife for sexual intercourse and she denied him, the angels would leave her until she responded to her husband's request. I thought if I said no to sex, that would give my husband more evidence that I couldn't be a good wife. I hoped the act would win me his favor, but I found myself mired more deeply. A few days later we argued again and he told a family friend that although we had "made up," I was still defiant and stubborn around the house. He had taken my words and my willingness to have sex as evidence that the beating incident was resolved.

I resigned myself to staying not so much out of love for my husband but because I could not bear the loss of the marriage. The thought of not being married meant major failure, and that was less bearable than being with a man who mistreated me. Because I had lived Islam as others defined it, when my husband used Islam to justify his actions I believed that something was indeed wrong with me. I couldn't cope with the rejection or the demise of a dream that had meant lifelong security and validation. As reality pierced my illusion and disappointment set in, I became angry and, as the therapist I was still seeing observed, borderline clinically depressed.

One short and intensely painful year later I was divorced and in the worst depression of my life. The last time I spoke with my husband, we argued, and he told me to "remember my place"—meaning my place as a woman. I had constructed my life around the ultimate goal of marriage, and thus I had nothing to anchor me. Though my parents, whom I lived with during this time, and my close friends supported me unconditionally, I felt intense shame and guilt about my marriage. I was humiliated and embarrassed. Each day I awoke, surprised that I was still alive. I suffered through my divorce because I believed that something was wrong with me. Somewhere along the way, long before I met my husband, I had internalized that those in authority defined my self-worth. If my intuition told me something to the contrary, it was to be ignored. In short, I had to subjugate my will because others knew best. "Others" could be my parents, my husband, or my community.

And one day I looked up, and Saleemah was gone. There was only a shadow of myself left behind. Gone was the outgoing, confident, and intelligent woman I had known. She was replaced with an angry, broken, not-good-enough-to-be-a-wife woman who was disillusioned because she'd lived as a good girl but didn't get the happy ending. The crisis of my marriage called my entire life into question. It was the dark night of my soul in that nothing and no one could ease the pain. Everything I knew failed me in this regard, and I could only turn to God. Upon reflection, I am grateful for my marriage. The end of that relationship marked the beginning of my quest for self-awareness and for God, free from the interpretations of others.

After the divorce my mother said, "Now you have a chance." It was a rich opportunity given to me by God to stop living through others. It was a spiritual depression designed to strip away my illusions and all that was false and to personalize my faith, relying only on God. While I understood this intellectually, it would take several years for the transformation to occur in my heart, and during that time I walked in fear and despair, still believing I was defective.

Shrouded in black, wounded but hopeful, I attended my first *thikr* (a session chanting remembrances of God) just before sunrise. The imam said "Welcome" as I joined the group. I introduced myself and his wife responded, "That's a beautiful name; what does it mean?" I said, "It means peaceful," and the imam said, "It actually means sound, as in without defect." It was as though God spoke to me through the imam, sending a message affirming that I was okay just as I was. I remember that early morning being a major turning point in my life.

In order to save my life, I knew the first step was to get Saleemah back. Except for the *thikr*, I stayed away from mosques and many of the Muslims with whom I'd grown up. Formerly, I had gone to mosques in search of spiritual nourishment and guidance and comfort. More often than not, I found myself distracted by the fire and brimstone sermons promising death and doom, or by someone disrupting my prayerful state to correct my dress or actions. Sitting in cold basements or behind opaque partitions with screaming children, pretending to ignore the whispers about me and my marriage, slowed my ability to heal. Though I'd grown up with this being the norm, I just couldn't bear it any longer as I faced my new life. I stopped going places and interacting with people who left me feeling judged and empty. I surrounded myself with my parents and my inner circle of close friends. I thrust myself into prayer and isolation, turning to a variety of sacred texts, self-help books and tapes, and holistic healing.

During this time my mother presented me with a wonderful gift. One day, half joking, she said, "Whatever your father and I have done to mess you up, let's discuss it and resolve it so you can move forward." With that statement, she gave me permission to acknowledge the issues of my upbringing so that I could move forward free from the burdens of my upbringing. I was fiercely loyal to my parents and found it hard to confront how they raised me. I didn't want to hurt them by discussing the impact of my upbringing. My mother's gift began a series of conversations through which I've come to understand my parents and appreciate their role in my life even more. Her gift freed my family to deepen our relationship.

In one of these conversations, my mother revealed to me that in her early twenties, prior to getting married, she had been assaulted at gunpoint. From the moment I was born, my mother was determined that I would be protected and that no man would abuse me as she'd been abused. The limits she placed on me were her way of protecting me from harm. Using Islam to support her methodology was a way of legitimizing it and making it beyond reproach. Unspoken for so many years, it became subconscious. Enlightened with this new understanding of the context of my mother's actions, I was free to transform my relationship with God and Islam and myself.

I began to reevaluate my life and specifically the rituals I performed. I decided to stop doing things that didn't make sense to me, so I stopped wearing hijab—not because I felt oppressed wearing it, but rather because I realized that I had never chosen hijab for myself. As I read the Qur'an and secondary texts on Islam and meditated on hijab, I realized that my spirituality had nothing to do with whether or not I wore hijab. My access to Islam was not located in my outer appearance.

During this time I worked with a pioneering magazine for American Muslim women entitled *Azizah,* which presents the accomplishments and perspectives of Muslim women in North America. After embracing this new consciousness of myself, I began to meet other Muslim women like myself. So few women of any tradition or tribe receive the necessary support when they go off to create themselves. I met extraordinary Muslim women who, like myself, strove to reclaim our God-given right to live self-determined lives, even if it meant being on the margins of the Muslim community. Through reading and prayer, I began to realize that by following others' interpretation of Islam, I had constructed my own prison and relinquished the rights God granted to me. I now have a profound understanding of *taqwa* (God-consciousness). I understand that *taqwa* has always been within me. What that means practically is that now, after years of surrendering my own will and voice to follow another's, if something doesn't resonate within me, I don't do it. I don't need to find proof in sacred text, because I already know it. While I appreciate the need to delineate the proof, I'll leave that to the growing number of American Muslim women studying Arabic, the Qur'an, and Islam so we can access the sacred texts and present a more gender-equitable and humanistic Islam.

Further, I learned that during the time of the Prophet Muhammad, women and men prayed in one common space, and that the Prophet allowed women to lead mixed-gender congregational prayer. The notion that women couldn't lead mixed prayer and were undeserving of equal access to the mosque and to voice within the mosque had seeped into my consciousness over the years. I'd never protested being relegated to a separate and inferior space in the mosque, nor did I request to lead prayer. My silence was my acceptance of this way. But now I knew that freedom was mine, and in June 2004 I marched with a group of women to reclaim space and voice in a mosque where women had been banned from the main prayer hall and from leadership positions. In reality, I marched for myself to reclaim the voice I'd lost years before.

My path to God has been filled with doubts, difficulty, and ease. The more self-aware I become, the more I feel that I am aligned with God's best plan for me. My faith grows stronger, no longer weakened by external forces. Islam for me is surrender to divine will, spiritual practice, and cleansing my soul of hatred, resentment, and jealousy. What I now know is that for me, Islam is fundamentally a way of life emanating from God's mercy. I have been endowed with the nature to live my absolute best life, and only I can determine what that means. The Prophet Muhammad taught us that "To know yourself is to know your Lord." And I am closer to my true self than I have ever been.

On my journey, I learned of pioneering Muslim women worldwide. Muslim women in America can look here and abroad to know that the movement is global. Women in India and New Jersey are building their own mosques, and there are female imams in China. Our sisters in France, refusing to be labeled by those Muslims who would judge them with misguided notions of honor, have authored a book, *Ni Putes Ni Soumises (Neither Whores Nor Submissive)*, protesting the mistreatment of women in the name of Islam. In South Africa a Muslim woman gave the Friday sermon, and in Chicago a Muslim woman led the *Eid* prayer.

This anthology is a collection of the stories of some of the American Muslim women who are on the front lines here in the United States. It is an honor and a blessing for me to present these women, as each has inspired and encouraged me. We are the future faces of Islam.

PART I # CROSSROADS

The women in this book were all raised primarily in the United States as Muslims. For the most part, we don't recall a time when we were not both American and Muslim. American Muslims can largely be divided into immigrants and American-born Muslims. In this first section we will see how these multiple identities intersect. What's it like to grow up Muslim in the United States? What was our relationship with mainstream society and with the Muslim community? Who were our role models in crafting an American Muslim woman identity and in personalizing our faith?

The first stories frame separately an immigrant and an American-born Muslim experience in the United States. These stories, told by the first American Muslim novelist of Indian descent and by a Harvard-trained historian, reveal the complexities of growing up Muslim and how our various identities—American, Muslim, female—intersect.

HOW I MET GOD

Samina Ali

I have an old square photo of my family that was taken soon after we arrived in Minneapolis, Minnesota, from Hyderabad, India. In it are my parents, my older brother, and me (my younger brother has not yet been born). It is December 1970 and there are three to four inches of snow on the ground, enough to cover our feet to our ankles. Just beyond our figures stands a snowbank that rises taller than my brother's almost two-year-old stature. It is night and I can just make out the blurry red of a traffic light, trees empty of leaves, footprints that have made a path in the snow. I am less than a year old and dressed in a turquoise winter coat with matching snow pants, red and white shoes. My brother wears an army-green jacket with a broad yellow-and-white stripe down the sleeve. My mother is in a gold sari, her thick braid running to midback of her gray wool jacket. My father wears nothing more than a brown cotton shirt and darker brown pants, tailored for him in India. None of us has on hats or gloves, though it must be minus-degree weather.

It is an odd photo, taken almost on the sly, capturing us at a moment in life when we are simply alive to what is within us, too disoriented by this unfamiliar land to pose. Because of this, not a single face is entirely perceivable. Both my parents are in pro-file, my father gazing down at me, while I am gazing down at the snow, my small hand clutched inside his larger one. My older brother is almost completely turned away, only the bottom of a brown cheek visible. Something off in the distance has caught his attention, a car horn, a bird, something he has not seen before in Hyderabad, a new and strange sight to behold. My mother seems to be staring at my father, but, when closely examined, I can tell she is really staring off at some thought. She is young, in her early thirties, about the age I am now. She looks haunted and alone.

"When we first arrived, I thought America was full of ghosts," my mother said to me twenty years later, when I was interviewing her on video for an undergraduate course I was doing on testimonial literature. She was my subject; I wanted to examine the trauma experienced by immigrants and what they do to overcome it and survive, some staying clumped in their immigrant group, other heartier ones actually assimilating into their new culture, a different way of life. My mother never really assimilated. She wore saris until I was in high school, at which time her Indian-Muslim friends imbued her with enough courage to switch to loose *shalwar-kameezes;* then slowly, eventually, on my prodding, she put on her first pair of pants and a blouse. My father's eyes looked ready to pop out of his skull when he came home that day and saw his wife in American clothes. He laughed in delight. My mother, embarrassed, ran into the kitchen to warm up his dinner. Every day she cooked a fresh Indian meal. At home, we only spoke Urdu. She never took a job out of the house.

So what did she know of America to say it was full of ghosts? In December 1970, when my parents emigrated to the United States, they signed a lease on an apartment in South Minneapolis. My father worked all day at an engineering firm, then, in the evenings, because his Indian degree wasn't fully recognized, he went to the University of Minnesota to redo his masters. My mother stayed home alone with two children. She had left Hyderabad and, with it, she had left her family, her friends, her community, her childhood, everything she had grown to know. A place of noise and chaos, of visitors coming and going unannounced and fruit and bangle sellers calling out their wares and imams bellowing the *azan* five times a day from each corner mosque, leaving dogs howling, goats bleating, and babies shrieking in sudden wakeful shudders. She had left behind servants and the comforts of language and religion. And, after a quick twenty-four-hour ride in an airplane, a hurtling journey into the unknown, she had landed in Minneapolis during the dead of winter. Outside her apartment window, the streets were empty but for a passing car, and all was silent. This was the land of the dead. And the figures that sometimes walked by, heads covered in hats, faces hidden behind mufflers, hands warmed by gloves and shoved inside jacket pockets, not saying a word to each other, to her, were nothing but ghosts. To keep her company in this desolate landscape were her two children, neither of them talking yet, and a black-and-white TV that barked at her in a language she didn't understand.

Yet 1970 was among the years when the United States was experiencing a severe shortage in professionals and so was luring educated people from foreign lands. India was among those places America turned to for help, practically handing out visas to all doctors and engineers. Osmania University in Hyderabad, where my father studied, produced many such professionals, and one of my father's classmates, a heart surgeon, came over to America a year or two before my father and settled in Minneapolis. It was that one connection, that one friend in the vastness of America, that one known and familiar face, which compelled my family to also settle there. Many months after they signed the lease on their apartment and got the first phone of their lives, their names and number printed in the white pages, a call came from out of the blue: another Muslim man from Hyderabad, also with his wife and children, also an engineer from Osmania University, also trying to make it in this bleak place ripe with the American dream. The loneliness and isolation had forced this other man to take up the phone book and go down the list of names, call each that he recognized as a fellow Muslim—our being Shi'a and the others Sunni didn't matter at that point—and speak in the language that still reverberated inside his skull, Urdu. Soon, twenty Urdu-speaking Muslim families from India and Pakistan were gathered together from across the Twin Cities and, in an old church, the first Islamic Center of Minnesota was opened.

★★★★

I met my two closest girlfriends from this community when I was four. One was the daughter of a doctor from Hyderabad, the other a daughter of a literature professor from Pakistan. We grew up together, learning to pray *salat* and celebrating our first Qur-'anic recital, our *bismil'lahs,* our first fasts of Ramadan. Together, we also sang our hearts out to Pat Benatar, had crushes on Simon LeBon of Duran Duran, went through the aches of adolescence, and complained to each other, far removed from our parents' ever-alert ears, of how isolated we had become from our American friends, unable to date or stay out past 11:00 P.M., and, because of this, unable to participate in many school events (none of us, for instance, went to prom). The only slumber parties we were allowed to attend were at each other's homes, because our parents knew each other from the Islamic Center. The older we got, the more aware we became of the inner circles of friendships at our schools that we, with our familial and religious constraints, could never penetrate. In Minnesota, where most people are tall, white, blonde, and Christian, we small, brown, Muslim girls stuck out. And our strange habits of celebrating Eid and not Christmas, of wearing heavy jeans throughout the humid Midwestern summers, of fasting for days on end in the middle of the school year, and sometimes of taking off to India for months at a time, made us even more peculiar. Whatever school friends we collected over the years at our three different schools were misfits themselves.

Despite this, not one of us would have traded places with the most popular girls in our classes. Our parents, being recent immigrants, cherished their Desi culture with such vehement respect and care that we children inherited their fierce pride for our backgrounds. Our parents identified so fully with being Muslim that we children understood from childhood how superior our religion was to others. Though we may have been misfits in the eyes of our American classmates, we knew, inside, that we were better (a belief reinforced constantly by our parents). Being South

Asian, being Muslim, was an honor. Only years later, while taking my testimonial literature course, did I discover that our parents' affiliations with Islam, their desperate clasping of a religion which some of them had little true knowledge of, was a way for them to hold onto their homelands of India and Pakistan, and, by extension, to their own childhoods, to their own upbringings, to their own former selves. Indeed, our parents were so seeped in nostalgia and loss that they made sure we children lived in what they themselves had, as cognizant adults, chosen to leave behind.

And just look at the country they had come to! In the 70s, America was undergoing a transformation itself: women's liberation, flower power, Vietnam protests, drugs, sexual exploration, and freedom. To our parents, this was the real chaos, a sharp contradiction to the calls to prayer, the arranged marriages, the orderly rules of family and community they had known. They felt the threat of American culture encroaching on our innocence, and to keep us protected, to keep us from being inhabited by America while we inhabited it, we children were threatened by expulsion, from family, from community, from Allah. A clear choice was set up, a reductive dichotomy: our way or their way, the chosen way or the lost way, God's way or Satan's way. This was not just Little India in Minneapolis, this was militant Islam in the kindest and most innocent of ways. Of course, we chose God's way, which really meant we chose our parents' ways. Indeed, even a decade later, during a few of those slumber parties, late at night, my girlfriends and I spoke in earnest of how lucky we were to have been born into our religion, for all those outside of it were born blind and would, by their own choosing, die blind—may Allah have mercy on them.

I can trace my strong sense of belonging within Islam back to grade school, when, during second grade, I told my teacher that I would no longer stand before the American flag to say the Pledge of Allegiance. "I am Muslim," I said, "and my allegiance is only to Allah." My parents, having been schooled in India, were not even aware of the Pledge I said each morning, but I imagined that if they were, they would certainly have protested alongside me. So at age seven, consumed by an intense internal struggle of good vs. evil, I finally spoke out. For about a month afterwards, while my classmates stood to say the Pledge, I sat in my seat and stared down at my desk. Eventually, my teacher, who I am sure had never before (or perhaps since) faced such a dilemma, came to me and asked me to stand. She had spoken with the principal, who had spoken with administrative and civil and religious figures, and they had all concluded that I could say the Pledge. "You are Muslim," my teacher said, "but you are also American."

American Muslim. It was the very identity my family and community feared, the two constructs seeming to them contradictory, canceling each other—canceling their children!—into negation. At that point, I stood, because I was a child obeying my teacher, but my heart was with God and, while the others made their pledge, I whispered *Surah Fatiha*. I thought, I am Muslim, nothing more.

Yet my understanding of Islam was limited to my community's teachings. Each Sunday, at the Islamic Center that our parents had founded, I took classes that taught me not much more than to recite *surahs* from the Qur'an, to memorize the Five Pillars, to know the biography of the Prophet's life and, though my Shi'a family didn't believe in them, to revere the four Caliphs: Abu Bakr, Umar, Uthman, and Ali. After classes, which were held in the basement of the old church, the men climbed the steps to the front of the building and entered the large prayer hall, where pews had once stood, to pray, while we women and girls climbed the back stairs to stand cloistered in an airless room where confession must have once taken place. This is the Islam I was exposed to growing up, along with a set of prohibitions: do not wear revealing clothes, do not drink alcohol, do not smoke, do not gamble, do not laugh out loud, do not call men's attention to yourself, do not talk during prayers, do not wear makeup, do not foster friendships with the opposite sex, and do not, whatever you do, have sex!

This last prohibition was a commandment in my household, which my mother must have whispered to me each morning before I went off to school along with the ominous threat: "If you do, he will know." She was referring to my future husband, the one my parents would choose for me.

"How will he know?" I would often ask, frightened.

"He just will. When a valuable vase has even the faintest crack in it, it's useless. Don't become useless, Samina."

The way in which she whispered her words to me, the way in which she guaranteed that "he" would know, along with the way men stood before us in prayer and, at functions, stayed huddled in groups far removed from women, began the first stirrings in me to see their power, which, because it seemed omniscient ("He will know") made me start to associate men with God. Once I did, I began to be conscious of how men's superiority over women was tightly woven into our parents' teachings of Islam: men were unerring and strong and all knowledgeable, while women—while I!—were folly-ridden and weak and prone to commit sin. Men were the enforcers of God's rules. Women were the humble servants. Men guided and protected women. Women were thankful.

My two girlfriends and I grew up believing that we were priceless vases that could easily shatter, thus shattering our family's reputation. We believed this would happen simply because we were women and acts of self-control were beyond us. Thus, we believed that we were victims to our femaleness. So while our brothers were encouraged to go off to medical school and become educated and successful, each of us was, at nineteen, married off to a man chosen for us by our parents, thus stunting our spiritual and intellectual and emotional growth. Sadly, because we girls had internalized our parents' fear of our own power of self-determination, we gladly gave up our freedom and entered into these arranged marriages with a sense of relief and, even, a duty to Allah.

The men we married were similar to each other: all three had grown up in India or Pakistan, all three were professionals, all three needed our citizenship to come to the U.S. In other words, our husbands were like our fathers: raised and educated there, living out their dreams here. Our parents plucked these men out of their homelands for this very reason: the daughter's purity should match her groom's, a man not exposed to and perhaps even controlled in some invisible way by demonic Western possession. In this manner, the daughters of the community became mere vessels of parental legacy. Our community's values and interpretations of Islam are what came to inhabit and control us, while our fathers wrote out our destinies.

Yet it is Allah who charts a soul's journey, and our lives will unfold in exactly the way that best facilitates our spiritual evolution. In looking back at my life now, I see that, as much as my parents wanted me to know God, so did I. As a child, I wrote notes to Him and slid them behind dresser drawers, in the back of closets, between folded clothes, places where only He could locate them. My notes were full of love for Him, gratitude, along with entreaties to keep my family and me safe, and, most importantly, to help me to be happily and solidly on the divine path.

Such innocent notes were in sharp contrast to the god I was being introduced to at home and in the community. That god, according to our parents, was to be known through prayer, fasting, recitation of the Qur'an, faith, good works, virtue, and a thousand other motions of devotion. The god we were bowing to was to be feared. He was omniscient and omnipotent, which meant we had to be mindful of not only our behavior but also of every thought. He was judgmental, meting out rewards and punishments, listening to some prayers while ignoring others, showing a miracle here while barrenness there—it all depended on our "goodness," and our goodness was an accumulation of good intentions and deeds.

Even at a young age I bristled at such descriptions of God. The God I knew in my heart was loving, compassionate, and merciful: "al-wadud, ar-rahman, ar-rahim." He was forgiving, "al-ghaffar." And He kept us on our right path, "ar-rashid." In other words, I never believed in the punishing god who had to be feared. Because I could not find this god outside of myself, I knew even as a child to keep my version of Him quiet.

Islam is a way of life, it is submission to Allah's will. Our main task as humans is to be strong enough to overcome our ego and allow the higher power to steer the course of our existence. There is no single divine path, as I had believed as a child; each of us comes here with a destiny of our own to be fulfilled, just as a flower's destiny is to bloom, a tree's to blossom and wither and blossom again.

When I was married at nineteen, I believed I was following my destiny, and I was. But not for the reason I had thought at the time. Then, still a novice on my spiritual journey, I thought my marriage would make me a devoted wife who would bear children and raise them to be Muslim, and these roles of wife and mother were, along with the other rites, my forms of devotion to Allah. But Allah had other intentions for me.

Soon after I got married, I discovered that my husband would never be able to have sex with me. He was physically repulsed by my body and, whenever he came close to me, he would have to rush to the bathroom to vomit. He blamed me, saying I was "too Americanized" for him. He wanted someone who was more "pure." Naive and still a virgin, I fervently prayed that Allah would rid me of any impurities I might be housing in my body so that my husband would consummate the marriage. I felt so ashamed and guilty over his rejection of me that I didn't confide in anyone. My secrecy only compounded the problem: in my mind I linked my husband's acceptance of me to God's forgiveness of me—not a farfetched notion, since I had been raised believing men were God's mouthpiece. As such, while I lived with my new husband and in-laws in Hyderabad until his green card was approved, I went to shrines and mosques and made mountain pilgrimages. Each time my prayer was the same: dear Allah, compassionate and merciful, forgive me my sins and reward me with this union.

My prayer was never answered. For the first time I wondered if my parents and community were right: God was vengeful. Why else would He be punishing me? My doom grew wider when, over the next few months, I discovered that while I was criss-crossing the city in hopes of finding a spiritual house from where I could get God to listen to me, my two girlfriends were happily married and zipping off on their honeymoons. I felt forsaken, and worse, I felt forsaken without cause.

Two years after I returned to the U.S. with my husband, he received his permanent green card and quickly revealed to me that he is gay. He moved to another state and began living with a man. From there, he sent me divorce papers. His confession was small and insignificant in the face of my three years of internalized self-hate. He had not only made me question my sexuality and womanhood but had destroyed my faith in God. His revelation now made me feel used in the most dehumanizing way, and I turned to God again and asked, "Why did you allow it? Why did you not protect me from him?" My marriage, after all, had been arranged only after conducting a series of *istakaras,* all of which had come out successfully. God, in effect, had blessed the union Himself—why had He deceived me?

If God's wrath were not enough, even my community, who insisted my husband was not gay, sided with him while making me, the girl who had grown up in their midst, the pariah: they said God was punishing me for my sins, which was why a perfectly good Muslim husband had left me. My girlfriends were still married to their men and all the women in the community were still married to theirs, which could only mean there was something wrong with me. Without material proof, they took my husband's rejection of me as spiritual proof that I was tainted. They said I had an American lover, that I was a whore, and that was why my husband had refused to sleep with me. Worse, they said that it was in order to hide my own disgraceful behavior that I was trying to ruin his reputation by claiming he was gay. All daughters in the community were ordered not to speak with me, while all parents silently turned away. My own parents were shunned, and though the religious division had never been important before, now it was raised against my family: Only Shi'a parents could have raised such a disgraceful daughter! I was so severely ostracized that my parents asked me to leave the state for my own good.

Around this time, the University of Oregon was recruiting me for their creative writing master of fine arts program, and not having any place else to go, I accepted their offer. For the first time in my life, at twenty-four, I was on my own, hundreds of miles away from everything that had formed me—parents, ideologies, culture, fears, limits. If I were to describe my transformation over the following two years, it would be to say that, as an insect does, I molted. Slowly, I shed the skin of my beliefs. I felt like my parents must have when they first immigrated to America: immersed in a foreign land. In Eugene, I did not know any other Muslim. Just like that, after a five-hour plane ride, I was on my own, outside any controlling forces. No mosque, no Sunday school, no aunties and uncles watching over me, no parents telling me how to dress. I could be whoever I wanted. I chose to be like the other students: single, carefree, still bumping along on the journey to self-discovery. I felt so betrayed by my God and community and family that it was easy to put them all behind. I told no one that I had been married before, that I was a pariah, that I was angry.

My anger pushed me away from God. Immaturely, I thought: If He can forsake me, I can forsake Him. That first year in Eugene was the last time I kept fast during Ramadan for six years. My *salat* also dwindled over the months to nothing. As any other American in my class, I met and fell in love with a man and moved with him, after our graduation, to his hometown of San Francisco. In our most intimate of hours, late at night, just as I used to confess to my girlfriends at slumber parties, I now whispered to him my secrets: I had been married before, I had lost faith. I continued to carry so much shame over what had happened to me, continued to see it as my sole responsibility, that I was convinced that he, too, would reject me. He married me instead. My second husband is white and atheist. My father, in protest of our union, didn't attend the wedding, didn't speak to me for three years. I didn't care. In much the way he had once controlled my destiny, I felt I was now controlling it myself.

When I was deciding to marry Tim, I saw the choice as between Islam and my writing, between religion and secularism. Although I had grown up always choosing Allah and what my parents considered "the right path," I now chose against God—or so I thought.

Right away, our marriage faced a life-and-death situation. His mother had been diagnosed with lung cancer and her body was in the disease's ravaging final stages. The doctor gave her six months to live. I approached the situation from my knowledge: she would die and go to heaven. It was her time. My husband and his family, however, smirked at what they considered my naive beliefs. There is no heaven, they said; when a person dies, that person dissolves back into the earth, becomes a part of nature's cycle. In other words, they did not believe in a soul.

This was the first test in my new life without God. In confronting the notion that a human does not have a spirit, I began to understand that I still held faith in Allah. In turning away from Him, I was being like a child that turns away from her scolding parents. But I had chosen this path and I wasn't about to go back just yet. My mother-in-law passed on a year later and her body was cremated, the ashes buried directly into dirt. No one cried. No psalms or *surahs* were said. A poster was made of her life with various photos. People spoke of their shared significant moments. The funeral was called "a celebration of life." How different from the Islamic burial, where the body is undressed and wrapped in a white sheet, returned whole to God as it once came from God, where women wail and men weep, where *surahs* are recited and Allah called upon to aid the spirit back to Him. This "celebration of life" somehow felt holistic.

The night of the funeral, at home in bed, I finally cried, both for her and for my acceptance that the body is without a soul. My belief in heaven and hell did seem childish and simple. The woman who continued to cling to those ideologies needed to be buried, along with her mother-in-law. Like that, I awoke in the morning a new person, now fully in my body, fully without God.

Life without God was indeed a celebration in many ways. Without old values haunting me, I could now invent myself. I began by indulging in those things I had previously shunned: alcohol, smoking, wearing sleeveless dresses. My husband and I bought a home in San Francisco and threw cocktail parties. We conversed with famous people about literature, independent films, travel to exotic places. We went dancing together and rolled in at four in the morning, passing the next day in a hazy, blurry stupor. We worked little and enjoyed a lot. But this life, though glamorous and adventurous, provided little inner fulfillment. Day after day, I grew more estranged from God until I felt nothing but a vast emptiness inside me. I had become, as my mother had once aptly said, a ghost in a desolate land. Life was meaningless, and to live each day to its fullest meant to live each day in full self-indulgence. Growth was reduced to that of material gain and increased possessions. I began to wonder why I was here.

Then I got pregnant. Bringing in new life gave my own flat one a new purpose. I was filled with a sense of joy and love and magic. I was in wonder over my body and its ability to create. I, a simple woman, was making life! The months of my pregnancy were peaceful months where each moment was infused with a sense of miracle. Sitting in my garden as I bathed my pregnant belly in the California sun, I would watch the bees penetrating lily stamen and listen to the neighbor's pregnant cat yowling, and I would think: there is a higher order to all this. What that higher order was I didn't know. I wasn't ready yet to return to God. Still, the connection I felt with nature, with each organism doing its part in this active universe, was undeniable. And it was reassuring. My heart began beating again as I felt my old child self come back to life, the one who wrote notes to whatever greater spirit was out there.

I heard recently that south of Santa Cruz is where the portal from this world to the next is located. This is why California is suffused with alternative ways of thought. Living here while pregnant, I now turned to Buddhism. Through it, I discovered that my husband and I were living a life of ego. We were on the endless cycle of desire, attainment, increased desire, which leads, in the end, to misery. Life cannot be filled through acquiring and seeking pleasure. Death must become one's best friend in order to teach us what is important in life. My studies in Buddhism lasted for most of my pregnancy, but there was one tenet that I couldn't follow: the complete and total elimination of ego. The ego was my best friend. It protected me. I couldn't let it go.

I turned to Sufism by chance. One day, browsing in a bookstore, I happened on a Sufism book in the remainder bin. I picked it up because it was cheap and, while paging through it, I ran across a passage in which the author discusses how the ego is given to us by God and, as such, should not be judged. Instead, it must be balanced with spirit. I bought the book. Now I realize it was God's way of guiding me back to Him, for it was the last book I read before I delivered, and I still remember the one line that changed my life: *Allah is waiting for you to widen your eyes and see Him.*

After reading that sentence, I put the book down and cried. I felt a huge outpouring of stagnant and repressed emotions rise up out of me. For the first time in my life, someone had said what I had known since girlhood: God is not high up in heaven, an entity to which we bowed and prayed and worshipped. God is all around us, within us, outside us. God is everywhere, no where. Right here. All I had to do was see Him. The best part was to know that just as I yearned to know God, He yearned for me to know Him. My body was soaked through with love, and I bowed to Him after many years and sang out my childhood prayer: keep me solidly on the divine path so that I may know You.

This time, God answered my prayer.

In delivering my son, I died. Twenty minutes after I pushed him out of my womb, I had a grand mal seizure, the worst one can experience. It sent me into unconsciousness. During delivery, I had complained of head and chest pain, for which the OB had given me Alka-Seltzer. Now the doctors worried something more than indigestion was happening. Hours after my seizure, I was wheeled down for a CAT scan, which showed I had two brain hemorrhages, one a subarachnoid hemorrhage, which is serious enough to kill most patients on its own. I had other things accompanying it: the chest pain was from a heart attack. I also had liver and kidney failure, pulmonary edema, cerebral edema (to such an extent that it wouldn't respond to medication and the doctors were about to drill a hole in my skull to release the excess fluid), single-digit blood platelet count, blood that had stopped clotting—basically, every organ in my body had either failed or been damaged. I landed in the Neuro-Intensive Care Unit and my family was told that if I was lucky, I would die. Otherwise, they would have to decide who would be my ward. I plummeted into a coma.

I have read that when people have a near-death experience, they see a blinding light and a beckoning figure. I didn't. The place I inhabited was of complete darkness. When the Buddha was asked about death, he turned over his bowl, meaning a darkness within a darkness. I was residing in that enveloping darkness. There is nothing there, no relationships, no ties, no love, no fear, no pain, no desire, no connections. And, in this way, there is peace. If the world can be described in positive qualities—attainment, attachment, gain, power—the world of God can be described in negation—undying, unchanging, unmanifest, unmoving, immeasurable, invisible, infinite. In God's world, in His presence, I was nothing but pure awareness, pure consciousness, purity.

I met God, as I had prayed to do since I was a child, and then He sent me back. My recovery is miraculous. My body is stronger today than it had been pre-delivery. My neurologist from the ICU says that in all his years of medicine, he has seen only three people who have suffered to such an extent only to return, but that I am by far the worst case he has ever had. He also says that he remains in disbelief that I am alive, especially without any trace of injury, and that my full life proves the existence of God.

One cannot meet God and return unchanged. In these past five years, I have continued my studies in religion and have discovered that, at the core, all faiths say the same thing: God is omniscient, God is compassionate and forgiving, God is love, God is right here and everywhere and no where all at once. He accompanies us all on this journey through life, this evolution of our souls. He is the breath within our breath, the light brightening our own.

Religious ideologies try to box God into rituals and customs. Growing up, I remember the severe judgment and competition in my South Asian Muslim community: they competed with each other on who prayed the most, who fasted the most, who did hajj the most, just as they competed for the biggest house, the most educated son, the most dutiful daughter-in-law. Faith, even there, became trapped in the ego. People seemed to be proclaiming, God is on my side, rather than humbly asking, am I on God's side?

I have moved beyond such labels, occupying the very space of negation that my parents feared, though in a radically different way. I am no longer Indian, Shi'a Muslim, daughter, woman, or even American, mother, twice divorced, writer. I am no longer just human, either. I am what I saw in that darkness: I am pure awareness. As my body continues this journey through the material world, I shall observe my life unfolding without fear. For, in the end, the charting of a soul's journey is unknown to us, so we cannot be scared nor judge what happens. We must instead live each day as the new immigrants I see in that old photograph: surprised by what life is offering up, aware of its beauty and magic and newness, accepting of change. Assimilating here means merging with Allah's higher intention for us, trusting that there is no right or wrong path, no good vs. evil, no our way vs. their way.

There is only one way to God, and each of us, each day, each moment, with each breath continues toward Him in the way He has set forth.

My own journey has freed me of a love and worship of Allah that seemed limited and superimposed onto me. Now my boundless faith in God rises from inside and yells out in joy: *I am! I am!*

TO BE YOUNG, GIFTED, BLACK, AMERICAN, MUSLIM, AND WOMAN

Precious Rasheeda Muhammad

I am young, gifted, Black, American, Muslim, and woman—a medley of identities and intercultural exchanges at a defining moment in world history. I carry the torch of an Islam predicated upon universal human excellence, to the chagrin of cynics who claim it impossible for the faith itself to do so, let alone someone of my ilk. Yes, marginalization is a challenge even for me, the daughter of revolutionaries. But I, like many before me, am a "movement child." Even while I am still struggling for traces of cool air—feverish with the need to personalize my faith in the face of my intersecting identities and what Islam means to me beyond what I have been taught and what I am expected to be —I have taken to heart the responsibility to carry the torch of this faith and, as a believing woman, to actively represent Islam through contributions to humanity every day that I live.

I learned the weight of suffering on the human spirit very early in my life. It made me ponder at a young age how people made sense of their lives through religion. I had a chronic skin disease my entire childhood that sometimes covered nearly eighty percent of my body, including my face and scalp. My mother would have to shave my head. My clothes would stick to me and have to be peeled off slowly. Sometimes it hurt to even move. I was treated cruelly every day at school for nearly sixteen years. I found it difficult to go on at times.

For this reason, I could never stand to see another human being suffering. When I was a chaplain at Boston's Brigham and

Women's Hospital a few years ago, I prayed with a brain-dead patient's grieving family, read from the Holy Bible for a male AIDS patient with failing eyesight, and witnessed a premature baby take his last breaths as he was baptized before passing away. None of these people cared if I was a Muslim and I did not care that they were not. I truly believe my own sickness was God's way of preparing me for leadership by humbling me, sensitizing me to injustice and opening my heart to tolerance.

It was not a foregone conclusion that I would become a historian specializing in the experience of Muslims in America. I attended a performing arts high school, majored in drama, and auditioned for Juilliard, winning numerous awards for public speaking along the way that would, unbeknownst to me, prepare me for my later role as a lecturer on Islam in America. In addition to studying religion in college, I wanted to be a filmmaker and produce feature films with Muslim American characters. While obtaining a Master of Theological Studies at Harvard Divinity School I considered going on to medical school, but instead I was humbled by my interfaith experiences as a student chaplain, putting my hand, literally, on the heartbeat of religious America.

While pursuing my aspirations I kept coming back to one simple fact throughout my personal journey: I could not find myself in the history books. Where were the in-depth stories of American Muslims? Where were the detailed histories, the women's views, the studies of difficult intercultural exchanges, the accounts of activists and the coming-of-age stories that put a human face on a religion's adherents, effectively not leaving them vulnerable and alone in times of crisis? How can anyone understand your plights if they do not know who you are?

Who my parents are has shaped me into the Muslim woman I am today. My parents are believers who came along at a time when Islam, as freedom, justice, and equality, offered sorely needed structural solutions to combat the terror of America's racism. Through their practical application of Islam, I learned to stand firmly for justice from my father and to be an innovative educator from my mother.

My father arrived in Boston, Massachusetts, from the Deep South as a teenager, and he immediately joined citywide efforts to bring dignity and respect to Black people in the area, eventually joining the Nation of Islam (NOI). By the time he was nineteen he had married my mother, marched with humanitarian and labor leader César Chávez, and become affiliated with the Black Panther Party, assisting in the takeover of a Brandeis University building by students frustrated with what they understood as racist policies. He even joined the militaristic Republic of New Africa (RNA) but was expelled because he wanted to be a Muslim, and the Islam the RNA was offering was more political. My father was attracted to the NOI because it offered a complete way of life. And although he had exposure to orthodox Islam as well, he had never seen Black men so powerful, so strong and confident as the brothers in the NOI. "All I knew," my father once confided in me, "is that I wanted to be like them and believe in God."

There is an old worn picture of my siblings and me in 1983 sitting excitedly around my mother as she reads to us from the Holy Qur'an. Education of children—the importance of which was taught to her as a young girl in the NOI's Muslim Girl's Training (MGT) and General Civilization Class (GCC), along with modest dress, household maintenance, sewing, cooking, and general etiquette—has always been a priority to her. Our house was filled with general educational and Islamic studies tools. There was so much to learn, I never wanted to sleep. I can remember being eight years old and hiding under the covers after lights out with a flashlight reading *The Autobiography of Malcolm X* and *Roots*.

Sometimes my mother would lug crates full of all kind of books and put them in a shopping cart to transport back to our house. She had charts and blackboards and would teach us how to pray, how to read the Qur'an and how to live our lives as Muslims. She often taught children in our kitchen, where they would sit sucking their thumbs and reading voraciously. She told me that her first introduction to the practical application of the saying "It takes a whole village to raise a child" came from her experience growing up in the Nation of Islam.

The Honorable Elijah Muhammad's transforming, black separatist Nation of Islam saved the lives of countless African Americans through mental, physical, spiritual, and economic rebirth. I always marveled at my parents' recounting of the community's self-subsistence that had nurtured my mother from the age of three and my father from the age of seventeen. The international community of the NOI had its own paramilitary unit, bakeries, Muslim imports, office buildings, apartment complexes, a jet, a fleet of trucks, a bank, restaurants, clothing shops, cleaners, schools, grocery stores, farms, nearly a hundred temples in the United States and overseas, *Muhammad Speaks*—the largest circulating Black newspaper of its day, which my father had both sold and assisted in printing—and followers that ranged from reformed ex-convicts like Malcolm X to world heavyweight boxing champion Muhammad Ali and Harvard college students like one of my uncles.

It is out of this historical context that my life began as a third generation Muslim in America. I have siblings, parents, a grandparent, aunts, uncles, cousins, nieces (making up a fourth generation of Muslims in our family), and close friends that I have known since childhood, all of whom are Muslim. I cannot imagine my life without Islam. It has shaped every aspect of my identity since the day I was born.

On February 26, 1975, a cold, snowy day in Chicago, less than a month before my birth, my mother sat in the balcony of a room filled with thousands of believers while my father, then a part of the Fruit of Islam (FOI), the NOI's paramilitary unit, stood on honor guard as Imam Warith (Wallace) Deen Mohammed, the son and successor of the Honorable Elijah Muhammad, was raised up high on the shoulders of several FOI. This celebratory moment marked the commencement of Imam Mohammed's leadership over the NOI upon the passing of his father just a day earlier. The Reverend Jesse Jackson, one of many nationally recognized leaders present, greeted the audience heartily with the universal greetings of Islam, *"As Salaam 'Alaykum!"* He told them the Honorable Elijah Muhammad was "the single most powerful Black man in the country and the father of Black self-consciousness." Then he said, "People are less because of his passing but more because of brother Wallace."

Reverend Jackson was right. It is because of Imam Mohammed that I was not born into the Nation of Islam but rather into true Islam as revealed to the Prophet Muhammad 1400 years ago. Without shedding a drop of blood, or giving in to the prejudices of race, he began to lead a revolutionary mission, on that very day, to uplift all of humanity with the dignity, understanding, and universality of Islam. And so my earliest memories as a child are seamlessly interwoven into my identity as a Muslim in the world community of Islam.

I recall fondly how my siblings and I would listen to the imam's radio broadcasts or get out of class and go right to the masjid adjacent to our Muslim school to hear his Friday sermons in Chicago. We had great fun with a statement in one particular sermon when the imam shouted, with force and severity, "How you gonna try to hypnotize my child with a pair of Mickey Mouse socks!" Long after that day, we repeated those words over and over, imitating the imam's voice with great delight. These are the little things that shaped me as a child, made me strong, reminded me never to worship images, to be a leader, not a follower, to not give in to subliminal seduction, and to understand the importance of recycling the dollar within a community that had been "downtrodden through the muck and the mire" of America's racism.

I could not have been more than five or six years old when I used to tell people, "Call me Bilalian," a name once given to the community by the imam to show how one can evolve from slavery to "dignified life," like Bilal, the Abyssinian slave in the time of the Prophet Muhammad who heard the message of Islam and would not let it go. Bilal later became one of the most significant figures in Islamic history. Imam Mohammed had hoped that the name would catch on with all African Americans as an alternative to being called "black."

There were many Saturday mornings when my father used to

have our entire family cleaning neighborhood parks. Instead of watching Saturday morning cartoons like the other kids, we were out with swing blades, rakes, weed whackers, shovels, and garbage bags contributing to the upkeep of the communities where we lived. It is because of this that I have never felt comfortable around Muslims who beat non-Muslims over the head with Islam yet never make a contribution beyond that which benefits Muslims directly. I was taught that a Muslim should do good works because that is what God has put in our nature, not because we expect some reward. When we do this with no ulterior motives, I believe our call to humanity in the name of Islam will be heard more clearly.

I can still see the great Muhammad Ali doing his magic tricks for all of us children. He would come to visit the students at Sister Clara Muhammad School in Chicago, where I attended fourth and fifth grade, and we would be overwhelmed with joy. He never put on airs. Here was this great man that sat just like us on the floor when it was time to pray. Those memories instilled in me a great sense of equality in Islam.

Sure, my experience as a Muslim growing up in the United States was peppered with prejudices against Islam and Muslims. Imam Mohammed talked about this the day he took over leadership of the community in 1975. He pointed out how sometimes people of our own race looked at us as "those old Muslims, those old Muhammadans, those old fools, those strange people." And indeed, children picked on me because I was Muslim, or "Mooslim," as they would put it. I remember vividly quoting the Qur'an to a fellow seventh grader who would not leave me alone about my faith. "To you be your way, and to me mine," I told him sternly in Arabic even though he could not understand me.

It did not stop there. A few Christian members of our extended family pitied us because we could not eat pork, or love Jesus the Christian way, or, due to modesty, "show our shape." My grandmother was ostracized from some of her family for years because she was Muslim. No matter how beautifully and colorfully our scarves were wrapped, people would sometimes ask us, "Why do you all wear those rags?" Once a doctor even asked me, "Don't you know that rag will make your hair fall out?" And of course, there was always the irritating assumption that we did not believe in God because we referred to the Creator by the name "Allah," which unbeknownst to those who ridiculed us for this perceived idolatry, meant "the one God."

Still, I had a strong sense of Muslim pride and a connection, I believed, to Muslims all over the world as my brothers and sisters. Those were exciting, innocent times. My biggest worries, in terms of Islam, were juvenile—like when was the next time I was going to get to hear the songs of Wilmore Sadiki, a traveling singer and musician in our community. At community events, we would sing along with him to songs like *Covered All Over, Allah Really Loves Me, Muslim Lullaby, I Was Born a Muslim,* and *Allah Did.* Years later, my siblings and I would fight over his tapes trying to decide who would get to keep the old tattered copies we had held onto since childhood.

Childhood's end awakened me to the tensions in the Muslim world. Whereas I had been taught that the only distinction between Muslims was that of righteousness, I suddenly found divisions based on race, ethnicity, gender, class, and issues of authority. My negative encounters with large populations of the children of Muslim immigrants, and African American Muslims who were from different Islamic backgrounds than my own, challenged the concept of community I had been taught was the very life force of Islam.

In college I often encountered Muslims who simply would not accept me until they put me through the third degree. *How had I become Muslim?* Explaining that I was born Muslim was not good enough. *Well then, where is your grandfather from?* Surely, in their minds, I could not be Muslim and also be African American unless I was Nation of Islam, so my grandparents must obviously be from somewhere else. What obligation did I have to tell people I barely knew that my parents were once in the NOI? Did they not know that there were many African American Muslims that had never been in the NOI? Why did it matter? *Oh, you are not NOI —what Islamic school of thought do you follow, then?* Saying that I was just Muslim was not satisfactory. Didn't I know that I couldn't be Muslim without following a particular school of thought so that I could determine how I should live every aspect of my life? This of course was pointed out to me by a Shi'a Muslim, who I am sure had his own problem with alienation from Sunnis.

How could I, an American-born Muslim, and a woman, with no traditional Islamic scholarly training, know anything about Islam or speak on its behalf? That was the question I soon became conditioned to expect. Whereas we should have bonded over that which we all believed and is certain in Islam, instead we were divided by that which is conjectural and has changed throughout the history of our faith over time, place, class, and culture. I was crushed. During those days, deluged with the representation of Islam from so many conflicting sources, I found myself left with an empty shell of a religion, struggling to get back to the Islam of my childhood that was more practical and compassionate. I had been so proud to be a Muslim my entire life, to stand up firmly for my Islam in the face of naysayers, only to be rejected by other Muslims. Who was I if I was not Muslim?

My community was not opposed to traditional Islamic learning, nor did it disparage the importance of the great Islamic sciences and schools. Imam Mohammed has sent men, women, and children to study Arabic and Islamic Studies all over the Muslim world. But Muslims are supposed to convey the message of their faith even if it is just one verse from the Qur'an. I had been taught to go directly to the Qur'an, to look at the life of the Prophet Muhammad for myself and use critical reasoning. That is something I could do immediately while continuing to pursue the study of Islam throughout my life. And so I simply refused to wait for Muslims to resolve their standoff between who should or should not speak for Islam while crimes against humanity were being committed in the name of my religion and anti-Islamic sentiments abounded.

Of course, I did not always cover my hair, or wear hijab, and I assumed that this was a major factor in why I was not accepted. But then, I traveled to countries in the Middle East and was shocked to find many instances of women with hijab walking arm in arm with women not wearing hijab. I have frequently asked Muslim women in the United States why we cannot be more tolerant amongst each other like this. I have often heard Muslim women say that a Muslim woman who does not cover has nothing to say about Islam to her. It is difficult for me to understand how this issue is used so abrasively as a means to determine the measure of a Muslim woman's faith.

My community created a culture of modesty in dress, actions, and speech, as opposed to just head coverings. When women did cover, the styles and colors were beautifully represented. We even celebrated modesty in songs like *Covered All Over* that elevated women who chose to cover as "*dressed in God's love.*" The words still reverberate in my ears. I believe this made young girls want to comply because of the way it was presented, and they felt they had a choice in the matter. Although some women chose to be modest without hijab, I never witnessed the alienation of Muslim women who chose not to cover until college.

I remember how I used to admire a picture of Sister Clara Mohammed, the mother of Imam Mohammed, who risked imprisonment to maintain the right to home-school her children so they could escape the inadequate and racist school system of her day. Her vision, to teach her own children, evolved into the establishment of the Muhammad University of Islam school system in 1934 and later became the Clara Mohammed Elementary Schools, now established in forty cities in the United States and Bermuda and attended by children of all races, nationalities, and religions. Her picture hung proudly on my grandmother's wall back then, and I would look up at her beautiful, flowing white scarf tied in the back and wish to be like her. Even though I was too young to wear a scarf, and due to my skin condition did not have much hair to cover anyway, I wanted to be like Sister Clara and the others in my community who looked so dignified. I would take everything from pillowcases to curtains and wear my little first grade self out trying to emulate them.

Two years ago, I shared a cab with a couple of Muslim sisters from Harvard and was shocked when the Muslim cab driver suddenly asked us, "Why do you wear hijab? Are you from America? Don't you know you are free here?" Although as a part of African American and Muslim culture I have almost always covered my hair in some style or another, I consciously chose to wear hijab in the past few years because I wanted to stand out unmistakably as a Muslim. Islam teaches that Muslims should distinguish themselves in dress and should be able to be identified as Muslims. Hijab, for me, was one way of doing that consistently. Hijab, as a conscious choice, gives me great feelings of serenity, security, and elation that being bullied into doing it could never deliver.

"I'm a Muslim, and therefore, by definition, I'm feminist," a young Muslim man declared during the 2001 Islam in America Conference at Harvard. The audience clapped incessantly, shocked that a Muslim man would speak up on the rights of women. It did not shock me. I learned as a young girl that Islam gives recognition to women's independent existence. In fact, my seventh grade teacher has me on videotape saying, "I want to be president of the United States of America when I grow up!" I always had social justice on my mind. Being a Muslim woman did not limit that. Once, irritated by a Christian girl in my tenth grade class who kept taunting me about Muslim women being oppressed, I flippantly told her that when I got married what was mine would be mine and what was his would also be mine, referring to the right of a Muslim woman to retain her property as her own even in marriage.

Strong Muslim women have always surrounded me. My mother used to nostalgically teach me drill steps performed by the MGT as she rattled off crisp chants and performed sharp about-faces, serious and tightlipped stances at attention, and militant to-the-rear marches. I knew then that "mommy" was not to be underestimated. As a young girl, I had Muslim women as Arabic and Islamic Studies teachers. I witnessed others lift their voices in spiritual songs and prayer in public settings. Men, women, and children even recited the opening chapter of the Qur'an in unison at the end of Friday congregational prayers, giving me a wholesome and deeply connected sense of community. Families were not gender-segregated during Muslim events. Women held positions of leadership in the community—in business, education, politics, and just about every area that Muslim men did, except that they could not be an imam. I could tell critics that women in Islam were not oppressed and actually believe it myself.

But again, leaving home for the first time changed all that. My subsequent experience as a Muslim woman was often of being the minority in a sea of women who had been raised differently. In many of these circles it was considered inappropriate for a woman to recite the Qur'an publicly at all, let alone in unison with males, or to sit with male family members during religious celebrations, or to pray in a room that did not have a partition, or to hold positions of leadership in mixed-gender Muslim associations, and the list continued. The women who were teaching me these things were well educated. They approached the understanding of these roles for women with vigor and firm belief. It was I who felt oppressed, not they. No matter how hard I tried to understand, I could not convert to this way of living. It did not sit right with my soul as a Muslim nor as a descendant of slaves.

I am from a people who have suffered greatly through the breakdown of the family line as the result of having chattel slavery forced on them. Segregation of the social space, in the manner in which it was being presented to me, went against the very grain of efforts to rebuild our communities and strengthen our family ties. For the first time in my Muslim life, I began to feel inferior and cursed to have been born a woman. I began to think, "Is this true Islam? Am I just really having a hard time submitting?" I longed for the days I could raise my voice in song with my community, singing words of uplift and social justice, without feeling as if I had committed a sin. But I need only have looked to the life of the Prophet Muhammad as a guide. In my studies and travels, I soon learned that how I had been raised was not out of line with that of the Prophet's time, where women had active roles in social and civic life and were not confined to such unyielding predicaments of social space.

Now that I am much older, I understand that the way I had been taught to determine how I should live my life, as a Muslim, was controversial and downright revolutionary. Many of my co-religionists outside my community were wading through centuries of commentary and interpretations, believing it to be outside of the boundaries of Islam to enter independent thinking into the equation. I had, in my innocence, burst through these closed doors and demanded to be accepted as "just a Muslim"; I had not waited for authorization to do that which I believed the Qur'an clearly told me I should be doing. Ironically, since September 11 many respected Muslim leaders have been leaning toward this approach, which Imam Mohammed taught us so long ago, as vital to the future of Islam.

"Sustained cultural relevance to distinct peoples, diverse places and different times," the esteemed scholar Dr. Umar F. Abd-Allah asserts, "underlay Islam's long success as a global civilization." Observing how Islam in China looked Chinese and how in Mali it looked African, he opined that for Islam to be successful in America, there was a need to develop a distinctly American Islam as well. Many Muslims are ignorant of the fact that this has already occurred in the African American Muslim community, which is constantly evolving too out of an authentic quest for an "Islamic self-definition" with "sustained cultural relevance" to the distinct concerns and histories of the African American people.

Muslims should view the success of Imam Mohammed, in his ability to navigate an Islam more true to its universal roots, as a critical part of their rich and complex collective history as Muslims and as Americans. For more than a quarter of a century, believers under his leadership, numbering in the hundreds of thousands, have made significant contributions to the betterment of American society—contributions ranging from educators and entrepreneurs, to judges and state representatives, to social justice and interfaith activists, to men and women in every branch of the U.S. military (including my younger brother, who is a Marine), and so much more. African American Muslims are not only the single largest ethnic group of Muslims in the United States, but they have also been the first such community to successfully bring Islam to the hearts and minds of the American public in a substantive way. There is much that we can learn from their struggles and accomplishments.

Education is the great equalizer. I believe that when we are knowledgeable about our neighbors as opposed to being afraid of what we do not know, we are more inclined to live together as one humanity, one global community, and to share in the possibilities for our posterity that universal human excellence allows. And so I have poured my heart into educating people about the growth and development of Islam in America, about the Muslim American experience, and I cannot stop now.

I once stayed in a rooftop hotel room in Fez, Morocco, listening to Qur'anic recitation on my headphones for nearly three weeks. When I finally checked out of that room, my skin was glowing like a newborn baby, my soul was renewed, and the ailments I had suffered from my entire life had gone into remission. Living Islam is a deeply personal, emotional, and spiritual experience for me. Sometimes I catch myself walking down the street praying. Verses from the Qur'an roll off my tongue unconsciously at first. "When comes the help of God and victory," I often hear myself whispering aloud in Arabic, and the tears begin to well up in my eyes.

Just a few years ago, I was a stubborn hybrid seed fighting to grow, not fully accepted by many of my American compatriots, because of my religion, nor by my immigrant coreligionists, because of my family's path to it. Nonetheless, I sprang forth from the fruit of my parents' Islam, taking root in a lonely and unforgiving American soil that would allow me no other option but to find myself on the world's stage as a leader. Imam Mohammed's words of wisdom have never been more potent to me than at this moment in history. "The salvation of society," he cautions, "and the survival of civilization depends upon establishing and preserving healthy, sound, truthful, and charitable leadership." That is the type of Muslim I strive to be every day that I live.

The Qur'an and hadith have many guidelines governing relationships. One will find many rules about interacting with friends, business partners, spouses, children, and so forth. Marriage in Islam, not unlike marriage in other traditions, is a multi-layered institution. Pressure to marry, layers of culture and patriarchy, notions of love and romance, idealism and expectations, dating, having and raising children in and out of wedlock, and power dynamics are some of the issues that come up.

In this section contributors discuss a variety of relationships and how they've forged relationships in an American Muslim context. And I would be remiss to present a discussion on relationships without presenting the dynamics of sex and sexuality. What choices do we make? Is there sacred text that we use to empower ourselves sexually? Do we demand fulfilling sexual experiences? What are our notions of our bodies, sex, intimacy, and sensuality? The subject of sex and sexuality remains a major taboo, largely not discussed in Muslim communities except to say that you burn in hell unless you do it with someone to whom you are married. If you are not married, the usual solution for addressing sexual tension is for parents to marry off their children in their late teens and early twenties and for couples to speed up wedding dates. Others practice celibacy until marriage, using their years of celibacy as a badge of honor. And others participate in sexual activity with varying degrees of guilt and secrecy.

Sex and sexuality is the elephant in the room that no one wants to talk about. Keeping sex and sexuality hidden allows dysfunction to breed unchecked. This dysfunction has meant that Muslims in America contend with sexual abuse, female genital mutilation, unfulfilling sexual experiences, and worse. It will take a safe and honest conversation about sex among Muslims at the family and community level in order to encourage Muslims to engage in sexual relationships and in conversations about sex and sexuality with a sense of personal responsibility and freedom.

This section explores love, sex, and sexuality in the lives of American Muslim women. A poet and an entrepreneur share thoughts about motherhood and about their marriages across racial and religious lines. A woman giving voice to disenfranchised women in war-torn countries reflects on how she relinquished her own voice in her marriage, and a Fulbright scholar remembers how she and her best friends found love. And finally, a courageous Muslim lesbian discusses her desire for acceptance from her family and community.

REMEMBERING LOVE

Sham-e-Ali al-Jamil

Don't ask me
whether I know
the Desi woman
married to the Black man
because we all don't know each other
and don't start
about when he converted,
we were both born
and raised Muslim.
What is wrong with converting anyway?

You question me
in hushed tones
about whether my parents
still speak to me,
feel entitled to ask
detailed questions
about my personal life.
Why would they stop
speaking to me? I respond.

See the speaker at the Desi wedding
praise the bride and groom
for preserving honor
by marrying within their
ethnic community,
then watch the hall of 300 people
applaud with delight.
The liberal intellectuals
clap alongside
the modest conservatives
in the name of purity.
Lots of talk about diversity in Islam,
but who is practicing?

Makes it easy to forget the
elderly man
in the city square
graying beard and
tasbeh in hand
staring at us.
When asked,
What are you looking at?
he said, taken aback
with tears glistening,
You both look
so happy
and in love
I could not turn away.

MY OWN WORST ENEMY

Manal Omar

There is a hadith of the Prophet Muhammad that says a person's worst enemy is between his two sides. As I reflect on my hyphenated life as a Palestinian-American Muslim woman, I realize how many self-imposed struggles I have had to overcome, and also that I have always been my own worst enemy. I imposed upon myself cultural and religious norms that I inherited from my family and community. Though unspoken, I internalized the message that being a quiet and demure girl was the path to being a respectable and pure woman, and that by the time I finished college I should have a husband. And thus I entered a vicious cycle of making mistake after mistake, trying to prove that I was something I was not.

What bothers me the most is that as far as I can remember, I have always been a passionate advocate for women's rights. As a child I would argue constantly with my parents about why I had more chores than my brothers. My mother would remind me that even the notion of boys doing chores at all was progressive in comparison to how things where back home in Palestine. That was never a good enough answer for me.

I've always believed in the power of women, and I dedicated most of my high school and college years to empowering young Muslim women along with myself. I would give talks about Muslim women's rights—especially those related to marriage. I always found it progressive that within Islam women reserved the right to place conditions in their marriage contract (a sort of prenuptial agreement) that were fully binding on the man. Whether it was a woman reserving the right to charge her husband for housework or a woman being able to request a divorce due to lack of sexual compatibility, it always instilled in me a sense of pride that our rights were guaranteed. However, I also realized that there was a gap between what we practiced and what we preached. I remember reading once that a person's professional life is also that person's personal weakness—an idea reminiscent of the Arabic proverb which says that a carpenter's door is never fixed. Indeed, this certainly proved to be the case in my own life. I became the mouthpiece and champion of Muslim women's rights, though I ignored my own.

With the observations of my upbringing and a desire to please my family, I set out to produce a husband that my family, my community, and I could love. The first was a man I'll call Cousin. I was seventeen years old and had spent the summer in Jordan with my family. Toward the end of my trip, my cousin's family asked my family for my hand in marriage. We told them that we would consider the proposal, even though my parents had always been against the practice of marrying one's cousin, nor did they want their daughters to marry before they had obtained a college degree. My confusion led to my silence and my silence became my consent. Somewhere while crossing the oceans, this "considering" became a promise, and I found myself semi-engaged by the time we landed in the United States.

I knew that neither of my parents would ever force marriage on me; however, at that age, all I really wanted to do was to please my father and make him happy. Cousin was a very educated and respectable man, and I somehow managed to convince myself that I could do the dutiful thing and marry him, even if it meant sacrificing other things, such as love, friendship, romance, and my youth. After all, to want such things in life and from a partner, always seemed naive and impractical. Women (unlike men) have a sell-by date when it comes to marriage, and hence it was essential to investigate all prospects for marriage. I soon realized that embarking on this relationship would be to build on a lie. I did not enjoy it when Cousin sent me letters and flowers, and I hated myself for hating him. I confessed to one of my brothers that the whole thing was a horrible mistake, and hence the family drama across the ocean began. Despite the engagement being called off, Cousin pursued me for two years before finally giving up.

Shortly thereafter, I went to college and completely avoided the subject of marriage. I made a point of having as little interaction with Arabs and Muslims as possible and instead joined the university forensics team. After graduating from college with a degree in international relations, I realized that I had a desire to get to know the other parts of my hyphenated identity, so I moved to the Middle East. I spent the first year in Jordan, where I worked as a freelance journalist, before accepting a job as an information and reports officer for UNESCO. It was the first time I really lived in a new place, with neither family nor friends nearby. I considered myself to be a devout Muslim and had never had any experiences with men beyond formal friendships—Cousin notwithstanding. This environment set the backdrop for the second man, whom I will call Baghdad Beau.

Baghdad Beau was the closest I'd ever come to love. At that time for me love was pure and ideal and had all the emotional appeal it has for a schoolgirl. I was in awe and had great admiration for this Arab male character. He was tall, rugged, and lean, and he talked endlessly and with great passion about Palestine. We were good friends at first, and slowly the relationship became romantic—and to cut a long story short, I panicked! For the first time in my life I felt like I was very close to deviating from the boundaries I had set for myself. At the same time I had become very unhappy with the United Nations' Oil-for-Food Program. In my mind, I could not justify the salary I was receiving, because I felt it took money from the Iraqi people. I resigned from the UN and left Baghdad. Baghdad Beau supported my decision, and he made plans to visit my family to ask for my hand in marriage.

My mother would hear nothing of Baghdad Beau. Not only were his parents uneducated, but he had over eight siblings. For her, the prestige of the family was at stake. My insistence on wanting to be with him was viewed as nothing but a rebellion and as a way to hurt my mother. Thus I realized that in order to attain the type of relationship I wanted with her, I had to embark upon the "correct" marriage with the "perfect" man.

True to his word, one month after I had left Baghdad, Baghdad Beau came to Jordan with the intention of asking for my hand in marriage and was shocked to find I was already engaged. Hence we move to a man I'll call Virgo-Texas-Psychophrenic (VTS).

VTS was a hasty move, and in hindsight a very poor decision. He was born under the sign of Virgo; lived in Texas; was religious, yet liberal; educated, yet fun; and we shared similar backgrounds. He had the mannerisms of an Arab man, but with his blond hair and blue eyes, he had the looks of an all-American golden boy. And last but not least, he had the parental stamp of approval. What was the logical and smart thing for a good, single-Arab-Muslim daughter to do? Marry him, of course! We had a fabulous engagement and I was without a doubt the envy of many women in Amman. Though it was a long-distance relationship, with me in Virginia and him in Texas, I began planning our wedding.

And then it all changed abruptly, and I am still not sure exactly how it happened. A part of me suspects that VTS was guilty of the same thing I had done—choosing me because his family approved of me, not out of any conviction of his own. VTS started to make odd comments about my hijab. He questioned why I didn't wear tighter jeans and why I couldn't find a smaller headscarf to wear. However, while encouraging me to wear more provocative clothing, he would also claim that women who did these things, or women who wore high heels and makeup, were nothing but sluts. He kept stating that women had to obey their husbands unconditionally. He started to complain that I did not have a job, and that women should be independent. So I went out and got a job—he kept complaining. I started my master's degree, but then he started to complain about that too, saying it was "unnecessary for women to be educated at that level."

Despite my views on women's rights, I decided to appease him. There was something embedded inside me that said a woman should make all kinds of sacrifices to please her man. His loyalty and affection were the reward. So I dropped out of the program. I could not figure out what he wanted. Did he want me to be a stereotypical Arab-Muslim woman? Or did he want me to be more liberal? As I realized the fallacy in the equation of sacrifice plus appeasement equals loyalty and affection, I finally realized that I did not care what he wanted. It should not have been about him, at least not to that degree—it should have been about me. So I called him and told him where he could buy quality clay with which he could mold the type of woman he wanted to be with.

Upon reflection, I can see that my experiences with Baghdad Beau and VTS are the reasons why Sequel (who became my husband) was able to enter my life with such ease. Despite all my friends' reassurances that Sequel managed to fool them as well, I cannot shake off the feeling that I walked right into the most painful time of my life, eyes wide shut. I felt guilty for not fighting for Baghdad Beau, and my parents felt guilty for being so adamantly against Baghdad Beau and for rushing into VTS; they did not want to be seen as always standing in my way. So Sequel was my choice and my choice alone, although to be honest, I knew my parents were not entirely happy with him. Sequel was an Iraqi—not the Palestinian that my parents had always hoped I would marry. He was eleven years my senior, and he was what my friends always referred to as an F.O.B. (Fresh off the Boat). For us, an F.O.B. was someone who was caught between the extremes of living as if he were back in his country of origin and desperately proving he was an American. It later dawned on me that he was actually an S.O.B. (Still on the Boat)!

The wedding was great. But in all honesty, we never got a chance to have a real honeymoon. The honeymoon was a tour of Italy and Greece, and although the scenes from Santorini to Venice almost make the trauma of the next year worth it, the reality is that it was a hollow honeymoon, which set the tone for a hollow marriage. The first red flag was when he asked me to start a load of laundry the day after the wedding, while we were waiting for our ride to the airport. I was eager to start my new role as a wife, so I initially responded and thought nothing of it.

There were many other red flags on the trip, including his public temper tantrum at Heathrow Airport that made me wish the earth would split and swallow me and his general air of indifference toward me each evening. A few days later came the bombshell. I remember every detail of that night, including the smell of coffee and the smoke that circulated in the small Internet café in Santorini. I was standing behind him as he checked his email, and noticed a message with the subject line: *answer to your question from Dr. Stephanie.*

The email was from a gynecologist, responding to his questions about how a man could determine if his wife was a virgin if she did not bleed. When we finally did consummate the marriage, I had only bled a bit. The overall experience for the first time was at best overrated, so I was quick to forget it. Apparently, Sequel had been disturbed and privately questioned my virginity, which to him was the very core of my honor. Dr. Stephanie wrote back, "The best way to know would be to ask!"

Initially I had been furious because I felt it indicated an absence of trust, the cornerstone of a new marriage. In addition to the distrust that it demonstrated, it also made me feel as if my identity as a Muslim and Arab woman had been called into question. Sequel convinced me that I should be eternally grateful that he was such a sophisticated and educated man that he was willing to overlook my defect. Further, I didn't understand why, if this had been on his mind, he had not simply discussed it with me. According to Sequel, only one in a million girls don't bleed, so he had every right to be suspicious. He also felt I was overreacting, since most Arab men would have demanded a divorce on the spot. Since he was so liberal and educated, he had investigated the matter first. In his eyes, I should be grateful that my husband was so open-minded. The sad thing was that a part of me knew he was right. Somehow, I followed his logical reasoning at the time, and he even convinced me to have a bit of gratitude as well.

One thing I have discovered is my incredible ability to suppress. I somehow suppressed that event, and convinced myself that things would get better as we lived together and were able to bond more. Over the first few months it became clear that I could never do anything right, and I was often scolded for forgetting to rinse out the milk carton before throwing it away or advised on the best way to slice an eggplant. My response was to try harder—the equation sacrifice plus appeasement wins loyalty and affection had not been fully deconstructed. Even with intimacy, things were not going well. When I asked him what I could do, he told me why I was not attractive. I tried harder—enrolling in a gym, joining L A Weight Loss, and cutting down my hours at work. This was not like my other relationships; this was marriage. I felt that everything that I could do within my realm to create a good marriage must be done. I was not able to see how unhappy I had become. So much effort was put into trying to correct the problem that my own state of being became insignificant. As my efforts became futile, I found myself spontaneously bursting into tears. I wasn't even allowed that, and was often told that just because I could cry didn't mean I was more miserable than he. Soon the tears gave way to bitterness.

But you would never have known looking at us from the outside. We appeared to be the happy couple, and many people envied me for having such a thoughtful and attentive husband. During gatherings he would rush to make me a plate of food and go through painstaking measures to make eye contact and smile or wave from across the room. Because of the dichotomy between our private and public lives, I began to be irritated by the public side of him and would often snap or roll my eyes. I am sure many people thought I was the one to blame, since I was so ungrateful for having the "perfect" husband. Looking back, I realize my subconscious started to rebel, and for me that public display needed to occur in our private lives where nobody was watching. So this time when he asked me why I didn't bake bread like his mother, I asked him why he didn't hunt and slaughter a goat like my great-grandfather.

Within a year, I knew I was unhappy, but I still had not given up hope and desperately thought of ways to change the course of our marriage. He threatened me with divorce over and over again. I later realized he did not mean it, but thought it would scare me into conforming. For my part, divorce had not entered my mind. I had managed to convince myself that this might be God's test for me in this world, and that my job was to use patience and make the best of the situation. If I took care of him, then that nurturing relationship would bond us more than intimacy or companionship would. But the problem was in defining how to take care of him—the standards that he placed always left me one step behind, and eventually I became mentally exhausted from trying to keep up. I kept telling myself that life was short, and that taking the moral high ground was more important. Eventually, I began to realize that a miserable life could easily last an eternity, and divorce became a real and viable option.

And then the day arrived that I was ready to act. It was the last day of the weeklong sculling class on the Potomac River that Sequel and I had enrolled in. It was a 6:00 A.M. class, and for me, being so close to water that early in the morning was heaven. Throughout the week, the instructor asked Sequel and me questions about Islam and about being Arabs. True to the suspicious nature of an S.O.B., Sequel interpreted this to mean the instructor was a member of the CIA or FBI. Having lived in the United States all my life, I was used to such questions, and on a number of occasions I have had complete strangers approach me in the mall or grocery store to ask all sorts of questions about my hijab and my faith.

On the last day of class my instructor asked me if it would be possible for me to meet him and his young son for coffee so that we could talk further about my culture and religion. Out of respect, I informed him that I would need to check with Sequel first. I was impressed with the instructor's desire to learn more, and was already thinking about people whom I could recommend to talk to him at a later point. I really did not think anything of it, and to this day I am haunted by the scene that erupted. I had what one might describe as an out-of-body experience. I could see myself on the dock—I was standing there in sweatpants, a long-sleeved shirt, and my hijab. My husband was yelling at me. The poor instructor was shocked and did not know what to do. He kept apologizing and saying that it didn't have to be a meeting over coffee, a simple phone conversation would be sufficient. I was mortified and humiliated. The scene fulfilled every stereotype of a Muslim woman that existed in mainstream American culture (except for the whole sculling thing).

I went to work that morning and dealt with the incident like so many other incidences before it—by ignoring it. When I got back home that evening, I received a phone call from my brother. He said he was very surprised by my actions that morning. Sequel had called him to complain about the incident. Naturally, Sequel's version of the story was very different. My brother was under the impression that the instructor had asked me out on a date, and I had simply approached Sequel to tell him that I would be going on a date with the instructor. I was not sure which was more infuriating, the fact that Sequel had manipulated the story to such a degree, or the fact that my brother, of all people, believed it. I was horrified that Sequel thought he could call my older brother and tell him that his sister needed to be put in check! I told my brother not to worry and that I would deal with the situation.

When Sequel arrived home later that evening, I confronted him and asked him why he had called my brother. He responded by saying that he felt he could no longer talk to me and that we needed help. With that I agreed; however, it was what happened next that was my final wake-up call. While we were talking, the phone rang. This is where I had my second out-of-body experience. The phone call was a response to Sequel's having called the training institute to demand that the instructor be fired. The institute explained that the instructor was a married man with children, and that he did not intend any disrespect. Then it was the instructor on the phone with Sequel. I could hear him from where I was sitting. He was apologizing profusely to Sequel, and explaining that it was his own ignorance that was to blame, and "not the fault of your wife." He kept repeating the final part over and over again, and I realized that he was afraid Sequel might take the incident out on me. The fact that I was able to see this as an observer—detached from the situation, because to be present was too painful—was the wake-up call I needed. I went upstairs and packed a bag. Sequel did not try to stop me. In fact, he even carried my bag to the car. I had walked out on him before, so I assume he did not take me seriously and thought I would be back. When I began to file for divorce, he knew I'd left for good.

After my divorce, I felt myself beginning to wither. I had always been successful in different aspects of my life, and to have failed in marriage was very difficult for me. With the failure of my marriage I feared that my dream of having a family of my own might never materialize. Moreover, I felt something inside of me had died, but I could not pinpoint exactly what it was. I knew it was not the loss of my husband, because if anything, at this point I had gained a new lease on life. I can honestly say there has not been one single day when I have missed him or regretted my decision to leave him. It was the best decision I have ever made. It forged a path for self-recognition and self-discovery. It made me realize that no matter how much I tried or pretended, I could never be anything but the hyphenated Muslim-Palestinian American woman I was. With this grouping came complexities and nuances that needed to be accepted, cherished, and loved.

During the divorce, as part of my healing, I continued to see a therapist, and I decided to throw myself into my work with women and development—I mean literally throw myself. I spent a month in Afghanistan for International Women's Day, working with a delegation of dedicated women who wanted to witness the effect of the war on the women in Kabul. I also planned to accept a job that would put me in Iraq right after the war. I stayed in therapy to make sure that whatever I did next was not reactionary, and that I was not running away from the bad experience. With the sessions, I realized how much I was actually running *to* something, and that my soul and spirit were rejuvenated by being able to take control of my life and do something productive.

The steps toward the divorce were the first to make me feel like I was being true to myself. My work in Afghanistan and Iraq provided me with more knowledge and experience and challenged me to the point that I realized I could accomplish more than I had imagined. On a personal level, I allowed myself the necessary time (thanks to night curfews) to reflect on my life and my choices. Throughout this time of contemplation, I have become aware that despite all the work that I do on behalf of women, when it came to my own personal life I didn't have the strength to work the muscle of my voice. The most basic example was the fact that I did not put a single stipulation to guarantee my God-given rights as a Muslim woman in my marriage contract. Even the most common rights, such as a dowry, or the right to pursue an education, or to be able to work, I did not include. I have led many workshops for young Muslim women about their religious rights within the framework of marriage and the importance of making stipulations within the marriage contract. Yet in practice, I was unable to stand up to the cultural pressures, which deemed stating certain things "offensive." Moreover, I realize that I was consistently playing the role of self-censor, stifling my own true personality. I tried to be something I was not. In an attempt to control and monitor my feelings and to behave appropriately, I have always been my own worst enemy, enforcing all kinds of gender-bias stereotypes on myself and building walls around my emotions.

The only thing that truly causes me pain is the grief and sorrow that my family has gone through, and I wish there was something I could have done to protect them from all of this.

One of the promises I made myself when I resolved to get the divorce was not to allow myself to go bitter. It is a hard promise to fulfill, but looking forward, I do have confidence that the right partner is waiting for me. But I will not be able to identify him until I have come to terms with my own identity and my own perceptions of marriage and what a husband should be. The pain from my marriage has forced me to look inward and to question what it is I am looking for.

The reason I was so hesitant to submit this for publication is that among Muslims there is a stigma attached to the discussion of personal relationships. A "good Muslim woman" should never have this many personal experiences with men. I also know the stigma that is attached to me as a divorced woman, but I feel the need to share my story, because I know many women are willing to live unbearable lives just to avoid such a stigma.

Looking back in hindsight, it is evident that most of the absolute values that I chose to live by over the years stemmed from the misinterpretation and misapplication of both my religion and my culture, which admittedly at times are not in synch. While I have suffered, I have learned many lessons and pray that they will be instructive to other young Muslim women. Most importantly, I realize the need to be true to and accepting of myself. My background as an American Muslim of Arab descent is an asset, and once balanced, it is the most powerful part of my identity. To deny one aspect of my character, instead of weaving together the different fabrics of my heritage and experiences, is to suppress the potential woman I can be.

Having worked in countries around the world, I am thankful that I live in a society where I had the opportunity to move forward with my life. I consider a bad marriage to be a near-death experience, and I wonder what effect this story would have had on me had I heard it when I was seventeen. I realize I have been given a second chance. With God's help, I want to make the most of it.

MARRYING A BELIEVER

Asia Sharif-Clark

My husband, James, considers himself neither Christian nor Muslim but simply a man who fears God. Over the past twelve years, our marriage has been an incredible journey. I've been privileged to share my life with a man who understands my commitment to my Lord, my marriage, and motherhood. James and I were raised in different faiths, solely by our mothers, and we are designing our own concept of marriage. Most Qur'anic exegesis agrees that regarding marriage, a Muslim man can marry a "believing" woman ("believing" meaning one who is Muslim or a monotheistic Christian or Jew). Conversely, a Muslim woman can only marry a Muslim man. The reason given is that the woman would be subjected to and adversely affected by the laws and customs of her husband. While I knew that this was the prevailing ideology in my community, here is the story of how this Muslim woman married a man of another faith.

We met at the State University of New York at Stony Brook, and it wasn't love at first sight. Since my junior year in college, I felt emotionally and mentally ready for a lifetime commitment, but I had no idea that my senior year would change my life in a way I couldn't imagine. We had mutual friends, but we didn't know each other well. We often saw each other in my dorm or the cafeteria, and he seemed like a nice guy. A few months earlier I had ended a relationship, and I felt the need to be unattached. With no interest in a relationship, I never imagined James as a candidate. During a group rap session, a friend explained that James was interested in me. I thought there was some mistake; I had given him no reason to show interest. My friends in the dorm had become my family, and I treated him more like a brother than a potential mate. There was no affection, just a "hey" when we passed each other. I was at a disadvantage. He had learned all about my views and ideas in our group sessions, and I knew very little about him. He smiled a lot but barely spoke.

Over winter break we saw a lot of each other, and for the first time in years I decided to listen instead of speaking. I learned more about him in two weeks than I had learned all year. I discovered that he loved and respected his family and that he truly valued friendships. We spent a year getting to know each other, our lives, and our families. It didn't take me long to be really interested in him, and I knew he was an excellent candidate for marriage, no question about it. Our daily discussions allowed us to address any concerns. And so we discussed marriage, children, Christianity, and Islam. We shared our family and life goals, and he understood how important it was for me to raise our children in Islam. With the major concerns addressed and with no fear, I called James at work one evening and asked him if next Wednesday would be a good day to get married. He said yes, and on March 7, 1993, we were married.

It wasn't difficult for my family to embrace him. My mom has always embraced all people, and her connection with others left a huge impression on me. I watched her develop lasting relationships with members of different faiths, ethnicities, and cultural backgrounds. When she met James it was no different. She admired his patience and kindness, and how naturally he became part of our family. It was as though he had always been with us. His faith was never an issue. My mom got what she wanted— a son-in-law who believed in God, feared God, and was good to me. She has never been disappointed, and our families and communities supported our desire to create a lifelong partnership. When we couldn't find a mosque to marry us, we considered a justice of the peace. At that moment, we found an imam who was open-minded and willing to marry us at my mom's house.

Getting married required arrangements, but staying married required strategy. Our marriage has been filled with strategy, negotiation, and communication; I like to call it "staying power." We knew our situation would not be easy and that we had to work at it. One of the early mistakes I made was trying to get my marriage to resemble my idea of a traditional Muslim marriage. I explained Islamic etiquette and gave James all the mechanics and procedures so he would fit in. What I hadn't done was given James time to become comfortable with my faith. I was overly zealous and came off as pushy. And thus, many times I'd arrive at *juma* prayer or Eid celebrations with my sons and no James. Instead of considering his feelings, I was defending my own. He wanted to be himself and I wanted him to be where I thought he should be.

I wallowed in self-pity until I remembered what Rasheedah, a family friend whom I've known for twenty-six years, often said: "Allah has blessed you with a wonderful husband who adores you." She has always helped me to cherish my life and has offered an Islamic perspective on whatever I was going through. This was a turning point in my marriage because I became aware of how blessed I was to have a husband who loved and supported me. I had been trying to make our marriage mimic my idea of a Muslim couple's marriage because I thought Allah would be pleased with me. I'd seen so many happy Muslim families and wanted what I thought they had. I knew I had to grow up and transform my relationship with Allah.

Awakened to my gratitude for James, I realized that Allah wanted me to be true to myself and true to Him. I reminded myself that I signed on for this relationship, with this man. What I had done was change the rules. I wanted him involved in Islamic activities to make me feel better, and that wasn't fair to James. He'd given me exactly what he proposed, and he'd been honest from the beginning.

If that meant that only my sons and I attended *juma* prayer, that was fine—I'd share the topic with James over dinner. It required a new way of thinking on my part, and I had to work at it. I've come to understand that when two people from different faith backgrounds marry, issues, which inevitably arise, need to be resolved early. Through patience and communication, we've worked through our challenges and left no issue unresolved. I learned to let James be himself and embraced our marriage just as it was. I stepped out of my own way and allowed our marriage to take its natural course. It has its own rhythm, its own uniqueness, and we simply go with the flow. We've tailored it to meet our needs and the needs of our family. As a result we brought our sons, Tariq and Rashad, into a home filled with peace.

Our sons have been the best teachers. They are naturally curious about our Creator and their place in creation. Tariq often asks, "How can I help Allah?" "Serve others, ask for guidance, and ask for forgiveness," I reply. They attend a public elementary school and participate in a variety of sports and activities. A few of their friends are Muslim, many are not. Our sons love Islam, they announce they are Muslim to all who will listen, and they don't hesitate to explain Islam's benefits. It's a sight to behold and makes me proud.

My work as a mother has been my most challenging and most rewarding role. Allah has given me the most powerful and influential job on the planet: mother. I foster God-consciousness and spirituality within Tariq and Rashad, and I understand that the principles I instill will be far-reaching and will last many lifetimes. As a mother, I provide more than food and security, I provide possibility. Right now, I'm their gauge for success. Helping them excavate their passions and navigate their way through this world, I try to teach them to do what they love, not what I love.

One thing that keeps me feeling great about mothering is giving time to me. I regularly schedule in "me time" to rejuvenate my relationship with myself. It replenishes my spirit and my relationship with the boys. When I feel renewed I give longer goodnight hugs. I give to myself and my spirit so that I can give to my children and my husband, and I am blessed to have a husband who understands my need for "me time" and my need for independence.

I am very grateful for James and our marriage because it keeps me sane and connected. Whenever I have a problem or concern, he says the same seven words, "Let me know how I can help." It's like music. He's the kindest man I've ever known. I'm in awe of his ability to give of himself. He gives to the hungry and to the needy. He's gentle with animals and kind to strangers. He's practicing more Islam than he knows, and I thank Allah for him every day.

I am grateful to Allah for so many reasons. As a child He gave me a mom who made me believe anything was possible for me, and today I live life without limitation. As an adult, Allah gave me a dad who's taught me to practice Islam with sincerity and consistency. As a woman, Allah gave me a husband who works, struggles, and laughs with me. Allah gave me children whom I protect like a lioness protecting cubs. I thank Allah for the opportunity to care for others, and I awake each morning saying, "In the name of You, Allah, thank you for allowing me to wake up and work for peace and productivity." Each day, I make a conscious decision to live Islam through motherhood, marriage, and work. I've been blessed for too long, and been given too much, to deny the favors of my Lord.

FINDING HOME

Sham-e-Ali al-Jamil

In this room filled with
late night dreaming
your cries wake me
again.

Was it the fifth time you woke?
Was it really 5:00 A.M.?

The scent of you,
fresh and safe
skin soft,
moonlight's caress on moving water.
The four-days-old of you,
bundled close against me.

Was it you inside me all along?
You within me?

When I learned
of your presence,
summer's gentleness
against my skin,
lavender lines that
revealed you,
the air gleamed bright
sky clear, open.

In my muscular nest
you nuzzled
swam in a concealed sea
urgently grew
beneath my heart.

You are here now,
in the last sigh of this night
drinking breast milk
near my heart,
close to me once more.
I curl around you fatigued
feeling some ancient story
coursing through me,
your warm breath
painting luminescent landscapes
against my skin,
fragile life in my care.

At this moment,
she swept over me
home did,
not the brick variety
or nation.
Though I searched for her
it was she who found me,
unsuspecting
we wept in the
serene yellow light
glowing sincere
exchanged stories
reconciled
She missed me.

Was this me?

Bearer of life,
birthing dreams
under the light of
the last stars shining
before daybreak
nourishing and protecting my
now sleeping infant
fluttering smiles of contentment
like sunlight,
my own belly full of
belonging
after finding myself.

FUMBLING TOWARD ECSTASY

Yousra Y. Fazili

I became interested in Islam after developing a crush on a young Sufi boy named Ammar when I was sixteen. Out of a young crush emerged an intensely personal relationship with God—one that I hold dear and one in which I feel fundamentally Muslim, before I identify myself with a gender, a nationality, or an ethnicity. In fact, the love of Islam which began with the love of a boy, grew to the point where I began to wear hijab—not because my parents forced it upon me, but because I saw it as a means to declare and claim a uniquely Muslim American identity. I wanted Islam to be the primary means by which I understood life and the way in which people identified me. Hijab was not a symbol of repression—sexual or otherwise. To the contrary, it enabled a unique sort of freedom. People assumed the best of me; I never had to worry about bad-hair days, and on the laziest of days, with nothing to wear, I could slip on an abaya. My relationship with God and my intense personal identification as a Muslim was a result of those years in hijab.

Until I met Ammar, I didn't care much for religion. I was quintessentially American to the point that I refused to learn my parents' native tongue, stating that this is America and I speak English, and if there is a second language here it is Spanish, so I will speak that, too. Who knew a good Muslim boy could be so cute? Ammar seemed to come from another world; he wore a turban and spoke damn good Arabic for a Desi boy. I saw the key to his heart was a great big dose of Islam, and I plunged in, full of inane lines like "Tell me how to do that special prayer again." I blush to think of it, though it happened all the time on the American Muslim convention circuit—girls seeing guys and "admiring their *iman* (faith)" as code for admiring their ass or dark smoky eyes. I soon lost interest in him, but ironically I never lost interest in the world of Islam he introduced me to. As a Sufi, his Islam was more fluid, more spiritual, and far more appealing than the Islam I had known—an Islam where women and men were separated by curtains and men seemed to enjoy more privileges of humanity than women. I use the word "seemed" because I do not think my reality, and the reality of many Muslim women, represents the true nature of Islam, which is one of gender equity.

I became fixated on the image of Rabia, a female Sufi renowned for her piety; she was the first historical Muslim woman I had heard of who was not famous for being a wife of the Prophet. Famous for her piety, she commanded the respect of both genders for her intense devotion to God. I fancied myself a modern-day Rabia, a woman whom men and women would look to for spiritual inspiration, touched by my piety and seeming disregard for this life. I sometimes think Rabia was a myth, an allegory of the feminine love we as Muslims can have for God, and a feminine myth that freed men from feeling emasculated by their own piety. Alas, I am no Rabia.

The best part of my relationship with Ammar was that it led me to seek a new interpretation of Islam through Sufi texts, alternative histories, and alternative exegeses of the Qur'an. And so, with my newfound Muslim identity, I became a "hijabi," American slang for a woman who wears hijab, the Muslim headscarf. With more knowledge about Islam, I later "de-hijabed." This is not an essay about what I chose to put on my head, but I mention it because it played a role in how I reconciled Islam and sexual expression.

Like all Muslims, I was taught that sex was reserved for married people. Thus, the struggle for us young Muslims full of hormones was to repress those natural desires until we met and married Mr./Ms. Right. Though we were taught to repress our sexual feelings, the idea of sex lay hidden in the shadows of Islamic etiquette. As soon as children reached the age of twelve in Islamic religion school, the sexes were segregated. At my mosque the genders were segregated with a thick curtain; the underlying reason for this was that all men were assumed to be sexual animals who would not be able to concentrate on prayer if they looked at women. I always found this insulting to men. This entire system was designed so men would never fear public sexual arousal. I also found it highly naive to think that women lacked a forceful sex drive and therefore would not ogle men at the mosque.

Ask the most liberal and conservative hijabi why Islam sanctions the wearing of hijab and there will surely be mention of the fact that Muslim women must be modest and unalluring so they are not seen as sex objects; they simply want to be seen as people. The problem I have always had with this reasoning is twofold. First, it is impossible to desexualize one's self—our sexuality is an integral part of who we are and a part of our humanity that Islam celebrates within the domain of marriage. Second, this reasoning takes all responsibility away from men and places it on women. Men are not taught to have self-control, but women are repeatedly instructed to dress and behave modestly so as not to arouse a man.

The problem with ignoring our sexuality is that we are left not knowing how to react to it. In other words, when we are confronted by something we have spent so long repressing, it is difficult to have a healthy response to what is life-affirming, natural, and a gift from God: the ability to love and make love. It is Islam's celebration of sex (within marriage) that happily separates us from other religions. And Islamic scholars have historically had frank discussions among themselves about the reality of sex both in and out of marriage. Tragically, scholarly and honest discussions about sex and sexuality never filter down to one's local mosque or to the local imam, and certainly never come close to our Islamic religion schools. And when young Muslims seek advice, they go to their peers because there are no safe spaces for adult guidance. At least this has been my experience.

Oddly, as a hijabi, my peers saw me as a source of spiritual guidance. The more I learned about myself and sexual expression, the more I came to give two types of advice when asked Islamic ethical questions: the textbook line (no sex until marriage), and what I would do (being a good Muslim is more involved and deeper than who you are or aren't kissing).

The first time I kissed a boy, or you could say a boy kissed me—I was devastated. I went home and wept for hours. I thought I was going to go to hell, that this was the beginning of a steady descent into a Godless existence. The next time I saw him, my adolescent love, I confessed all my fears. He admitted it was awkward to kiss a girl with hijab, to reach to touch her hair only to find cloth—a reminder of the forbidden. It helped that we were both Muslims, and not children—I was eighteen and he was twenty. And yet, the result of my guilt and his understanding was more kisses, only this time more excited, more exploratory, bolder, and more ambitious. Again there was a cycle of guilt and prayer and seeking forgiveness from God for this divine sin, and then the next cycle of kisses.

We would meet furtively. While our friends suspected a relationship, no one ever said a word, and we were equally discreet. This was my first kiss, my first relationship, and later my first heartbreak. I did not have my mother's lap to cry in when there was tension, and I did not have my sisters to talk to, because sexuality for Muslim women, whether here in the United States or abroad, is a taboo topic.

As I mentioned earlier, my de-hijabing was coupled with a new understanding of Islam. The more I learned about my religion, the less I came to believe hijab was *fard* (obligatory). *Fard* is often contrasted with acts that are classified as *sunnah*, or following the traditions of the Prophet but not compulsory. I believed that the hijab was *sunnah;* I did not think it was something I had to wear. In addition to my personal epiphany was my intense study of the sources of Islamic law and hadith. Three books were crucial to my intellectual development as a Muslim woman: Leila Ahmed's *Women and Gender in Islam,* Fatima Mernissi's *The Veil and the Male Elite,* and Al-Tabiri's *History of Islam.* The first taught me to reexamine assumed norms of *jahiliya* society (*jahiliya* is the term used to refer to pre-Islamic Arabian society) and to reassess the radicalism of the Islamic revolution in seventh-century Arabia. The latter two led me to reexamine the Qur'an and hadith regarding women, hijab, and intergender relations in Islam. What became apparent from my foray into the world of Islamic academia was that our religion had been far more liberal in its past, and that our current understanding of Islamic norms gives primacy to hadith and exegesis over the word of God.

It was then, at nineteen, that I de-hijabed and decided to live my life with the Qur'an itself as my guide, not a jurist's understanding of the Qur'an as advanced by a particular *madhab.* (A *madhab* is a school of Islamic thought.) Armed with this understanding of Islam, I was able to explore my sexuality without the previous burdensome guilt and panic attacks. This is not to suggest that I had sex with every man I could find. In fact, I still think the Qur'an is very clear that one should not have sex until marriage. Islam is a religion of moral obligation to one's self, to society, and to God. I suppose my own understanding of Allah is of a God with infinite love and infinite kindness, a God who knows what is in our hearts. More than anything else, my God is a God of mercy and my God is a God of compassion.

An amazing thing happened in the summer of 2000. As if to welcome the new millennium with an uncharacteristic optimism, my two best friends and I (the wonder triplets, as we liked to call ourselves) met the men who would become our first loves. Our loves reveal the different ways that we, as Muslim women, reconciled our views on sex, virginity, and marriage. We each defined a stereotypical type of woman, akin to the ladies of *Sex and the City,* masking our search for love and husbands with adventures in dating.

Sarah met Michael in Syria when they were both studying Arabic at an institute. Sarah's family is originally Arab, and Michael is the white American our parents fear we will bring home. Sarah's asexuality was unique. Throughout college, she never kissed a man; dancing was the most erotic activity she undertook. At twenty-three, the world was hers for the taking. Lovely and tall, she had long, brown hair and a slender figure topped with a buxom chest. Despite the fact that she wore miniskirts and tank tops, she prayed five times a day like clockwork. It's hard for most people to understand that we Muslims don't fit into boxes.

Michael courted Sarah with sincere friendship founded on their shared academic interest in Arabic poetry. They would talk at school, through an afternoon tea, and into the night, long after we had all been bored to tears. They talked endlessly, ceaselessly, using intellectual discussion as an excuse to spend time together. When he first reached out to hold her hand she withdrew, startled by the warmth and the tingling sensation she was unfamiliar with and afraid of.

Isn't this only supposed to happen with a Muslim man? she wondered. If she could fall in love with a non-Muslim, could she not also fall out of love with Islam? What did that say about her? And if she could fall in love with a white man, was she not also turning her back on her culture? But she had never felt this—this beating of her heart, this flame that leapt up within her. After only two months of friendship Michael professed his undying love in a sweeping, romantic gesture on the beaches of Latakia. Sarah was confused. She couldn't kiss him. She couldn't say "I love you" back. She stuttered, "You aren't Muslim," like a sigh, like a lament, like a wish. You aren't Muslim.

He reached for her hand. She was hesitant. He was patient. The sunset turned the sea golden. Finally, she gave him her hand, and they walked the length of the beach in silence. After they each returned home from Syria, they kept in touch through email and late night conversations whispered over the phone. Was this love? She was so confused. You aren't Muslim. It was a lament. But he could become Muslim. It was hope. And so he did, and he came to meet her parents, who were charmed by his wit and sensitivity. He is Muslim, she told them. He is white, her father reminded her. It is love, her mother said, and so it was. And it was final. They married idyllically and Sarah, true to her beliefs, was a virgin even after her wedding night. They took it slow—the kisses, the caresses, sleeping together, and he waited patiently because this was love.

Aisha met Omar at the Harvard gym. She was running on a tread-mill, trying to get under a nine-minute mile, and he was lifting weights, trying to escape the stereotype of the skinny Indian boy. He saw her working out and came over to introduce himself: "Hey, aren't you doing research in the lab next to mine?"

"Why yes, yes, I am," she said, batting her eyelashes and sticking out her hand.

"I have been meaning to introduce myself," he began, buoyed by her smile. "If you are new to Cambridge, maybe I can show you around—being a graduate student is very different than life here as an undergrad."

"I would like that," she replied, smiling with her eyes.

It was the first time he had ever been so forward, the first time she had ever said yes to a date with a virtual stranger; the fact that he was Muslim somehow took the edge off the strangeness. Aisha is so beautiful, she stops men in their tracks—her delicate features, the creamy caramel skin and thick, straight hair, almond eyes, and delicate hands. Though often complimented, she was asked on only three dates throughout four years of college because men, assuming she would reject them, never bothered to approach her, preferring to admire her from a distance. Interestingly, Aisha had no problem with sex before marriage. To her, virginity was not the marker of a chaste woman; honesty and sincere devotion were.

On their first date they went to Shakespeare on the Common. Boston Common was lovely in the full, lush green of summer. Omar had brought a blanket and a Dean and DeLuca lunch basket, complete with wine and a selection of cheeses—why not make it a Bollywood moment?

"I don't drink," she apologized. He was embarrassed. "But I don't mind if you do," she was quick to add. She still can't remember what play they saw. All she could remember was the scent of his cologne (Acqua Di Gio) and how she prayed for a kiss, tingling when their arms brushed against each other and when their hands happened to overlap as they stretched out on the lawn to watch the performance.

Aisha and Omar became seen as the power couple of Harvard graduate school, destined for marriage, though neither talked about it because both would like to think they were leading lives less ordinary. Their parents had met, each refusing to admit that their children were dating but secretly happy that they had coupled off with someone from the same religious and cultural backgrounds.

Four years after they began dating, Omar's mother grew dangerously ill. By then, Aisha had become a part of the family. Omar's mother called them to her bedside at Beth Israel.

"Ji, Aunti, we are here," Aisha said holding the hand of the woman she had come to think of as a second mother. The hospital smelled of death and ammonia. Aisha tried to focus her attention on something positive. The hand in hers was wrinkled and yellow, dialysis machines glowed and breathed an eerie mechanical hum that rattled Aisha's concentration.

"Baiti, I know you love my Omar, I know you will care for him when I am not here."

"Hush, Aunti, you will be here a long time."

"Or not," his mother replied. And they all knew the answer. "He is my only child, I need to see him married so I can die in peace."

And Aisha knew it was right. Yes, he was her only lover, though she never planned it this way. She wanted her monsoon wedding, with five days of celebration and joy, not this air of death and sadness. "Think of it as an air of peace," Omar said. And it was understood. They married at the hospital so his mother could see that her son had settled before she died. A year later they had Aisha's monsoon wedding. And a year after that they had another monsoon: twins.

I met Abdullah at a party in Zamalek, an upper-class neighborhood in Cairo. Neither of us were supposed to be there. I was dragged by my friends, unhappy and pouting since I had just been stood up on a date. Abdullah, a Sudanese man, had been living in Egypt since 1990. He was tall and skinny, with eyes the color of honey and a closely shaven head. When he first approached me to dance I refused, not because I have a religious objection to dancing with men but because I hated the song. As the party progressed, my friends left, but I stayed because I had my eyes set on a young musician. "As long as he is here, I am here," I proclaimed.

At around 2:00 A.M. a fight broke out. Too much alcohol and too many men, especially Muslims, will often end in a brawl. Most of the people left the party, but my young musician was still there, and so I stayed. The apartment had two large balconies, each beautifully decorated with rows of candles along the edge. Going out for fresh air I found Abdullah on a balcony, smoking. We talked for ten minutes and then parted ways. Another fight broke out—some classic argument about a girl, two guys, and a look. Abdullah and his friends left to break it up. Later, Abdullah came back to ask for my number, and to my own surprise I gave him my real number.

He called the next day. That's when the enormity of what I did hit me. I gave my number to a stranger! He asked me out! This is so *haram* (sinful)! What if he's an ax murderer! At college I was comfortable dating because there was a zone of comfort knowing you went to the same school, but in the real world there was no such zone. I agreed to meet him at a mutual friend's birthday party. He looked handsome, and I looked lovely in a cream dress. My green eyes were lined with kohl and my Allah necklace and hand-of-Fatima evil-eye charm hung, as always, from a gold chain around my neck.

When we entered the club, Abdullah put his arm around my shoulders. At first I was ready to shake him off—I mean really, who did this guy think he was? But then my anger stopped before it could be voiced. The minute our bodies touched it was like a million little explosions all over my body, pure electricity. It was not that a man had never touched me; I was not like Sarah. But never had a man's touch produced something this intense, moving this fast.

We danced all night. And then, like Aisha, we broke the rules, and when he dipped me during the last song of the night and tried to steal a kiss, I let him. We spent all week together. The relationship was so different from anything I had experienced in the United States. In the States, a Muslim-Muslim relationship was filled with months of playing games, searching for meaning in intimate clues like the manner in which someone says your name, and then trying to fit your relationship into a halal framework with marriage as the ultimate end. It was so refreshing to date someone who wasn't American but was still Muslim. He wasn't burdened by our paranoid view of religion as a zero-sum game. We simply enjoyed each other's company and an intense chemistry, kissing beneath broken streetlamps and overhanging palm fronds in a city where an unmarried couple could rarely find privacy.

And though marriage was the last thing on my mind, it soon became the most obvious direction in which we were headed. As with my best friends, he also surprised me with a romantic overture that astounded me. On the one-month anniversary of our first date he arranged for us to have a special night out. After a lovely dinner we went to his friend's apartment, which had graciously been left vacant for the night. When I entered it was like a dream, the room was filled with candles and roses, wall to wall, floor to ceiling. Abdullah stood in the center of the room, handing me a letter. As I read it, my eyes filling with tears, I pinched myself to remind me that this was real. In the letter he said he loved me, it's foolish to love someone so much so soon, but it's true and he understood if I did not feel the same way, too. I remembered something my aunt had told me: "When you find The One, you know, and if you are with a man for more than a year and don't know, then the answer is no and you are too afraid to admit it to yourself." I looked up from the letter.

"I love you, too," I said.

"Don't say it if you don't mean it," he responded.

"No, no, I mean it." And we kissed.

But then I stopped and stated, "Abdullah, I am a virgin and I will be a virgin till the day I marry."

"You are?" He was incredulous. I was insulted. What do people think of us American girls? "I'm Muslim," I said, somehow forgetting that all of his lovers had been Muslim also. "No, I mean really Muslim."

And it was funny that my American Islam would be more "real" than their Eastern Islam. He was so happy he swung me around, proclaiming that even if I begged for it, he would never have sex with me, to keep me pure. My inner feminist wanted to take back my words because I was upset that he was so delighted I was a virgin. And I was also upset that I was so upset that he was not. We kissed like we could not kiss on the streets of Cairo, we kissed like it was the beginning of a new life. And it was.

Out of respect for personal privacy, some identifying characteristics have been changed.

ON THE EDGE OF BELONGING

Khalida Saed

This is also one of those things girls get hospitalized for, like masturbating.

As long as I can remember I have teetered on the edge of *something*. I have not always been an American. Sometimes I wasn't a Muslim. I never wanted to be a lesbian. But I have never had any doubt that I didn't belong fully in any of these identities. I teetered on the edge of belonging to the lesbian community and being invincible within it, on the edges of being American and Iranian, and on the edge of Islam. I have been juggling several identities all of my life, and it never occurred to me to complain at first. It seemed that the less I complained, the less people would notice that I wasn't fully part of their community—and community is the reason for everything I do.

When I was fourteen, I came out as a lesbian to my mother. Her response was typical. She was distressed. She wove God/Allah into her arguments and ended the whole thing with "It's a phase." She also hit me, and cried, and locked me up in my room. I missed two days of school. The most compelling argument she came up with was that I was far too Americanized and that my sexuality was an offspring of the American values I had internalized. This last argument may or may not have a ring of truth to it. I'm not sure I would have had the balls to discuss my sexuality at all, or even consider it, if my American side hadn't told me I had the right. Discussing matters of the vagina certainly isn't very

Muslim-lady-like. My mother and I have never spoken about it since. I was horrified at having hurt my mother. Honestly, it never occurred to me that my personal sexual orientation would hurt her. I was THAT naive. Our relationship today is as close as it can be when two people refuse to bring up the pink elephant in the middle of the room.

We are not unlike many American immigrant Muslim families. Sexuality of any kind is not discussed. She would have been more supportive of me if I had never come out to her at all and we had left it unsaid all of these years. Sex has been the one issue we cannot get over as a family. Sex has been the one "condition" in the unconditional love parents are supposed to offer their children. A woman's virginity is the most valuable bargaining chip she can bring to marriage. And she *will* get married one day, or else it reflects badly on her entire family and ruins the chances of marriage for her younger siblings. Bringing up lesbianism was the ultimate form of discussing sexuality. Not only was I talking about sex, but I was refusing to participate in the biggest institution religion ever created: Heterosexual Marriage.

"They don't have jobs, they live on the street, and they want to be men, for God's sake!"

My mother holds some of the biggest stereotypes of what a lesbian is supposed to be, but I don't blame her, because her notion that queerness is a strictly white Western construct is not that far removed from what my own ideas had been growing up— I believed that if I were to live successfully as a lesbian in America, I had to cut my hair, listen to Melissa Etheridge, despite my own musical tastes, and put aside my political priorities in favor of gay civil rights issues. There were no lesbian-Middle-Eastern-Muslim-immigrant-female role models in mainstream America. There were barely any female role models at all. I could hardly leave my own house without interrogation from both of my parents and my older brother, so I didn't have access to the Lesbian, Gay, Bisexual, Transgendered, and Queer (LGBTQ) youth community where I might have found a need for my voice and my unique experiences. There was very little for queer youth to do in New York City if they had a 4:30 P.M. curfew on weekdays and needed special permission to go out on weekends.

The dominant feeling I remember from those days is extreme loneliness and isolation. I deeply regretted my sexuality. It was a death sentence on my family relations. I knew that when I grew up, I would have to choose between my family and my own life. In my culture, choosing anything other than family is considered the epitome of selfishness. No compromise can be struck. I remember my mother saying that people "loved themselves too much." I began to equate self-love with anti-Islamic principles. People who loved themselves too much could not live within the confines of Islam and family. So I did the only thing I thought would make my family happy. I began wearing a hijab and started a Muslim Student Association in my high school.

I collected all the signatures, organized all the meetings, and when it came time to hold elections, I dutifully let all of the men run for president and vice president even though they hadn't done the work. A good Muslim woman never expects glory or credit, or so I thought. I was extremely proud of my ability not to dwell on not having been nominated for office or credited as the founder. I thought I was on my way to becoming fully Muslim and belonging to that community. But I never managed to stop being queer.

Every time I get a new girlfriend, I have to introduce her as my best friend to my parents. They think I'm very social.

I met "Jane" while I was active in the Muslim Student Association, and she became my first girlfriend. She was a junior in my high school; I was a freshman. She was my first kiss. We held hands and kissed for about a month before we broke up. We pretended to be devastated, but since we hadn't told anyone we were together, it was a nonevent, like all of my other relationships with women would be until I left home. Jane and I also did something much more important to me at the time than kissing; we went to some meetings for youth at the local Gay and Lesbian Community Center. I barely remember Jane, but I remember the meetings. When I first walked into the room, my heart stopped. There were about forty kids sitting in a huge circle. It took about twenty minutes to go around the room and state our names and ages because kids kept taking up too much time and giving out all of this information about themselves. There were a lot of boys with names like "Tanshelique" and "Diamond." I loved every one of them. As my turn to state my name approached I remember being very nervous and not knowing what to say. Should I give my real name? Should I state my real age? And when it was finally my turn, I blurted out everything about myself that I could possibly remember. I think I even included my middle name and place of birth. We all had a need to be known by somebody. I felt like I had a real chance to find someone with whom I could share all of myself.

If you wear lots of makeup it will make you look sixteen, then the truant cops won't pick you up, but the lesbians won't know you're a dyke ...

School time was the only part of the day where my family couldn't dictate what I did, whom I spoke to, or whom I loved. I began cutting school to seek out places with other queer youth. This meant going into the East Village and maneuvering around the drug addicts, the cops, the truancy police, and the drug pushers. My grades began to slip. I had prided myself on being a straight A student, but suddenly none of that mattered. All that mattered was belonging, and I felt that on Christopher Street. I hated nights because when the streetlights came on I had to go home. I became extremely depressed as my life became increasingly volatile and abusive. The stress of being poor and minority and of having a family to raise took a huge toll on my parents. They were scared of losing their children, and they had every right to be. By all definitions we were becoming less and less Iranian and more and more New Yorkers every year. Our grasp of our own language was dwindling, and we had lost our accents completely. I equated all things Iranian and Muslim with being anti-gay, and therefore anti-me, and those messages were reinforced by the mainstream LGBTQ movement. My sister regarded all things Muslim as completely foreign to anything she was interested in.

My parents tried to control us through fear and anger. There was no attempt to bridge the gap between religious and cultural identity and sexual orientation when I was growing up. No one was doing that work for youth. I did not realize it *could* be done. Thus I rejected Islam in all of its forms because I could not find a place for myself in Islam. I left the Muslim Student Association. They wouldn't allow female leadership anyway, and I had started the damn thing! I felt completely isolated in the world. I was extremely depressed and desperately wanted to find a way to be all of myself somewhere. I felt that I embodied the word "foreigner" everywhere I went. So when it came time for college, I left home.

Being gay and Muslim? That's like sinning automatically, for no reason, all the time!

While I relished the freedom, it came at a hefty price. My entire extended family was shocked because going away to college when you're female and Muslim is a contradiction no one ever gets over. It's simply not done. I was the first in my family to do it, and I felt as if I had fought my way there and through college alone. It was the first time I lived and interacted with people with whom I had nothing in common. My first taste of the dorms away from my beloved city and away from my family was horrible. I faced racism, homophobia, and worst of all, defeat. Out of my loneliness came independence, which was the best thing that ever happened to me. I learned how to survive.

When I was twenty years old, I found a website on the Internet for the Al-Fatiha Foundation. I was horrified. The website featured a rainbow flag with a star and crescent. It was the symbol of Islam against a *very* gay backdrop. It was a national group for LGBTQ Muslims, and it was unapologetic. I immediately shut the computer down and walked away. I revisited the website every day for an entire year, and I pretended to be horrified each time. In 2001, my girlfriend dragged me to my first Al-Fatiha conference in Washington, D.C. I was petrified, but I felt like I was finally being honest with myself.

One of the first people I saw was a huge man who looked like he just stepped out of the pages of a hadith. He had a huge presence and reminded me of all the imams from my past. I would later find out that he was the first openly gay imam. This didn't comfort me at all. I wanted to turn and run. I don't know what I expected from a Muslim LGBTQ conference, but I had not expected an imam. My girlfriend held my hand, but we didn't actually join the conference until the next day. I needed that entire night to build up my confidence. Mostly, I was terrified that it would not live up to my expectations. This was my last hope of finding someone to tell me that it was OK for me to be who I was. I didn't know how to reinterpret the Qur'an so that I was included. There were so few mentions of women and even fewer positive ones. I had no patience for the religion anymore. I didn't understand why I was a sinner when I obviously came wired this way. I don't remember a time when I didn't love women. I didn't make the choice, but I was supposed to be punished for it. I didn't want to hear it again. I didn't want that message validated for me. But I was equally not ready to hear that it was OK to be a lesbian and be a Muslim woman. I didn't know how to do that even more than I didn't know how to stop being guilty.

When I finally joined the conference, it was a wonderful and soothing and spiritual experience. I don't think I lied about who I was once the entire time I was there. I even prayed more regularly than I have ever prayed before in my life. At the time, I found it hilarious that the one time I found myself totally holy and totally Muslim was when I was at a conference for Lesbian, Gay, Bisexual, Transgendered, and Queer people. I stood side by side with men and women and prayed. Leaving that carpeted hotel room that served as the mosque for the conference was like leaving Mecca. I felt shocked that I could be that affected by religion when I wasn't really looking for it. I never found that feeling when I was looking for it in mainstream Islam. I felt cleansed.

I joined the board of Al-Fatiha immediately because I wanted to give that same feeling of belonging to other people. It wasn't enough that I had reconciled my sexuality and spirituality; I had to demand it for other people as well. I had heard that people in Al-Fatiha received death threats and harassing emails and phone calls. I had heard that it was dangerous, and I certainly felt a sense of danger even being at the conference. I was not scared of other people in the LGBTQ community; I was terrified of other Muslims. Being a member of Al-Fatiha includes speaking publicly, creating community for people all over the United States, finding funding for all of the conferences, and making sure that women and youth are heard. Al-Fatiha restored my faith in Islam because it included women in its leadership and insisted on inclusive prayer spaces where women were not relegated to the basement and forced to wear hijab even if they did not wear them normally. Women were even encouraged to lead prayer.

This was the Islam every woman dreams about. It is also the Islam that made the most sense to me. Progressive Islam operates under the belief that anything that sanctions discrimination against anyone is anti-Islamic. It is the belief that working toward social justice is an integral part of religion. It is the branch of Islam that is distinctly American and definitely a better fit into my life. I realize that a lot of what I had been attributing to Islam is really a byproduct of my own culture. Patriarchy and sexism are not necessarily Islamic traits but are actually cultural traits. Realizing this has allowed me to give religion another chance. I have also been empowered to begin reinterpreting the text outside the confines of sexism and homophobia. This sense of renewed life and spirituality is the biggest gift given to me from Lesbian, Gay, Bisexual, Transgendered, and Queer Muslims.

So you don't want to get married? What did you waste all that time going to college for, if not to be more appealing to a husband?
My family has come to terms with my decision not to enter an arranged marriage. I am in my midtwenties, which is ancient in my culture. I am in a wonderful relationship with a woman I met during college. I never saw myself in a long-term healthy relationship with another woman. She comes from a very supportive and loving family that has embraced me over the last three years. She challenges me to be more expressive and more of myself. She encouraged me to attend the Al-Fatiha conference, and I joined Al-Fatiha's board of directors with her support. When I was voted co-chair of the organization, she celebrated it with me, and when I received my first death threat she crawled under the covers of our bed with me and we told each other stories until it was safe to come out. She has gone out of her way to study Islam, Farsi, and Iranian culture so that she can understand my struggles and the choices in life. I have studied African American culture and history to understand her experiences. We have a love that matured gradually. I take her with me whenever I travel, and she takes me with her whenever she travels. When we are apart, we call each other three to four times a day. And like all good lesbian couples, we intend to stay together.

Last year we decided to get married (that gay imam would actually come in handy), and I wonder what I'll tell my family. I have no real hope of ever having them support me the way that they have supported my brothers and sisters. I want to marry my partner. I really do. But I'm not sure how joyous that day will be without any of my family. If I invite all two hundred of them, I might get one percent to attend, but I would risk my safety on the wedding day and the safety of my partner and her family as well. I'm not sure what the point of a public ceremony is without the public acknowledgment of family. Who would speak my native language at my wedding? Who would bring the bad traditional music? Who would cry for my lost childhood? So I delay my wedding year after year. It is hard enough to be in an interracial relationship, and then being lesbians, and being young, and being a Muslim immigrant in the post-9/11 era, and being so decidedly American in Muslim society . . . it's all so complicated and difficult to negotiate.

I would be really excited if I could have just one community to belong to in my everyday life. The LGBTQ community has a lot of racism work to do before we can be fully accepted as a couple and as individuals in it, and the Muslim community has tremendous homophobia work to do. I have decided to work on the Muslims. They are the group most important to me and most precious in my life. Al-Fatiha is the vehicle that I am using to accomplish this at the moment.

In my heart I secretly wait for the day when I will gather up my courage, walk into my mother's house with my head held high, and ask her to sew me a wedding dress, just like her mother sewed hers. And while we're on the subject of fantasy scenarios, I imagine her wiping tears of joy from her eyes as she leads me to the sewing machine to take my measurements. She will then do the customary passing down of jewelry. She'll take out my grandmother's pearl set that her mother gave her on her wedding day and extend it to me, saying, "You know, I always liked that girlfriend of yours. Tell me more about her mother and her family."

PART III

THE STRONGEST OF FAITH

Americal Muslim women are in the forefront of Islam's global transformation. In June 2004, I marched with a group of Muslim women to reclaim our right to space and voice in the mosque where many of us have traditionally been banned. That single act placed the role of women squarely in the national debate.

From the boardroom to the bedroom and everyplace in between, Muslim women have become change agents creating new paradigms for leadership and activism. In this section, a Ph.D. candidate, a corporate attorney, a university professor, and a veteran investigative journalist discuss activism and leadership, ultimately explaining how they've realized spirituality through these activities.

A DAY IN THE LIFE

Su'ad Abdul-Khabeer

3 a.m. Labbayka

My mind fumbles for words
So my soul may speak.
Labbayka Allahuma Labbayk
I surrender.
Labbayka Allahuma Labbayk
I submit.
Labbayka Allahuma Labbayk
I am captivated.

Like the first time,
Pray, like the next
I know
Labbayka Allahuma Labbayk
For you
Labbayka Allahuma Labbayk
I am here
Lord, I am here.

5 a.m.   Prayers Clothes

Allahu Akbar. O Allah!
did my sleeve slip as I raised my hands to pray?
no. yes. Maybe...
"When in doubt, don't do," so I
don't start over or don't not start again?
This debate exhausts me, Satan trying to wear

me down to focus on the minute, like what I wear.
Thoughts of length eclipse attention to distance from *Allah.*
Pulling sleeves to knuckles, stretching the limits of cotton again,
So more than every inch is covered, in my struggle to pray.
Allahu Akbar. Damn! This scarf may unveil necklines as I
bend in *sujjud.* Start over? Yes? No! Breathe. No. but maybe

it would be easier if I wore that huge scarf; maybe.
Then I'd be covered from brow to thigh, able to wear
Anything I like (under it) except these pants I suppose I
Don't believe *Allah*
is that particular nor rigid is the Lord I pray
to. But then again

fallibility is humanity, I could be wrong or then again
created with *fitra,* inclination toward divine Will, maybe
I am right and if it consumes me as I pray,
circular monologues on what I wear,
could be that *Allah*
wants me to let it go. Wants that I

stop delving into intricacies of complexities that I
can never answer; where no human is sure because again
only Allah
knows and maybe
then I can shift focus from clothes I wear
to wearing humility when I pray.

Please pray
for me. That I
move beyond the wear
and tear of doubting again and again.
Transcend maybe
and know Allah.

That I pray as if I am with Him again.
No matter what I may be
Wearing on my body, my soul will be sincere before Allah.

9 a.m.   Connotations of the Crown

some of my sisters
are in combat
with ideas newly born
and words older than the world;
yet, to cover or not to cover
Is not my battleground.

Because
among His signs is
watching your sista
hi-jab
the painstakingly smooth way
she pins, wraps, folds, tucks
her crown into place.
Because I wear it well,
this divine design.
whether wrapped high
or draped low and wide,
what better garment
for a Queen
than her crown?
And a beautiful person is a Godly thing.

To cover or not to cover
Is not my battleground

They'd like to paint me
unseen
with a veil gagging my intellect,
while in truth
the whole world is clocking
this invisible woman.

Young men in fitted caps
whisper
"Damn"
deep in sly glances,
Others offer courtesies in appreciation.
Women honor us openly or
with their arrogance,
And the press
can't get enough of us.

See, clothes do not hide the woman
They announce her.

To cover or not to cover
Is not my battleground.

This is no Grimm tale;
Covered women are not housed in storybooks
nor shielded by them.
When the cutest new skirts
Are mini
And mine
is scratching my ankles.
When Hakim
married the non-Muslim
with the perky breasts,
And Ali to the
Sister without a scarf
but great jeans/genes.
And I am branded
"religious."
When they only offer scarves
studded with restriction,
the rear masjid entrance,
and a stay home free card.
Then,
I don't feel beautiful
and I am.

Still whether the boys love me
the girls hate me
the Muslims castigate me,
To cover or not to cover
Is not my battleground.
For this scarf is
Simply, a blessing.

And which of the favours of your lord will ye deny? °
Not a one.
I am the world's most visible creature
and His most beautiful.

Mobile Muslimahs

What has
Southern legislators
and the heirs of Napoleon
cowering?

a woman.
a woman and her scarf.

Behold!
I stand
a woman and my scarf.
Now what's so scary
'bout little ole me?

Is it my brown skin
phenotype for criminality
cordoned off in
Banlieus of France
Ghettos of America;
that's got lawmakers
taking a nine to liberty?

Or is my crime
in the Color,
Faith,
of my scarf?

° Repeated verse in Chapter 55, Ar-Rahman of the Holy Qur'an

En le français et en l'anglais
liberté, égalité et fraternité
are trumped
by Sécurité.
"Security of the secular!"
is the rant of wing-tipped
white men
but democracy has been hostage,
at least,
since 1776—
so who's the barricade for?

And their mani-pedi
consorts
talk smack,
frontin'
like they kick it
with freedom on the regular
their angular
sentiments
under the guise
of liberty.
Free yourself!
they tell me,
patting my hand
tugging my scarf,
From the tyranny of Faith—
So . . .
I can be neatly chained
to a thong?

If you had asked me
I would have told you
I don't have any brothers,
My father rarely prays
and when he does
It is for my happiness
and my scarf
did not come with detachable weapons
nor dyed with subversive messages.
No.
My scarf
is about
Claiming space.
but you didn't ask.

★ ★ ★

Don't know why
they be fearing us.
Guess Mobile Muslimahs
be hazardous
to national security.
'Cause they can't see
the color of my hair,
when I strap a bomb to my Nike
and walk into a crowded mall—

Nobody wants to see another building fall.

I wasn't on that plane
I am not guilty.
Will not apologize for
someone else's insanity,
their pain.

Not a criminal
by virtue of my scarf.
Not a criminal
by virtue of my religion.
Not a criminal
by virtue of the color of my skin.

Will not modify my faith
to make you more comfortable.

If you had asked me
I would have told you
I am a woman
and this is my scarf.
I believe in God
and freedom
and work for a world
where that is possible,
Invincible.
And if that frightens you

Be Afraid.

1 p.m.   Rooftop Masallah

Unseen and Unheard
Must be, how you want me to be
As you build walls
Between me and my Lord.
Unheard and Unseen
Must be, how you need me to be
As you stifle my spirituality.
But unseen and unheard
Are the traditions
You use to stake your claim.
That organ between your legs
Is not designed to give you more privilege
To His Space, His Time, His Words.

Allah says His Earth
Is spacious,
Yet you rob me of my space
Space which should serve
As a spiritual haven
You have turned into crowded corners
With barely enough room to believe.

Must be, you fear me
Because you know
This deen is dangerous
Giving the foolish idea of
Dignity.
Making Allah the only Master
Making Allah the only Master.

So you can build walls
High as mountains
And continue to make
My corner smaller,
But you will not rob me
Of my right
I shall return
And each time
With the Qur'an in one hand
And a bulldozer by my side.

Despair

I hate them
b/c they have Jhirmack
    Bounce Back
Beautiful Hair.
I hate them
b/c their size
            is always on sale.
I hate them
b/c they are   perfect
and I am not.
I hate them.
I hate them
b/c I can't stop
craving
to be prettier and
            thin
prettier and
 thin and
 thin and
 thin.

Perfect shoes
Perfect bag
Perfect jeans
Perfect jacket
Perfect frame

in a world perfectly made for them.

illusion is what I cling to
b/c
reality
takes
too
much
energy,
and I am tired
of fighting
for space in this world
for recognition
the ability to exist
in my own skin
on my own terms.
I am drained
drowning
In false desires.

5 p.m.   Hijab Story 2

Got up this morning
soooo excited!
Yesterday,
I bought
the most,
Perfect pair
of jeans.
Finally!
my thighs are held
in a loose embrace.
Perfect sandblast
to my purple sweater-tunic
and lavender-purple-plum scarf.

Perfect jeans fit perfectly
but the sweater was a
casualty of the monthly.
Yet I remained
modesty in motion
(as they say)
and thus
my lavender-purple-plum sandblast day began.

At breakfast
my mother's eyes
read
"that shirt could be a little longer."
I smiled
and went to the car.

Reaching the annual community expo
where speakers rant to periodically filled auditoriums,
merchants sell out of Hamza Yusuf tapes
and 5 dollar scarves
Sister "so and so" greeted me
whispering between cheek kisses
"pin (kiss)
your scarf tighter (kiss)
a turn of your head (kiss)
a glimpse of your neck. (smile)."
I smiled broadly
and responded to the *adhan*.

After prayer
Sister "I don't know you from adam"
said

"Sister,
you can't pray in pants."
I began to smile but was interrupted with
"pants never conceal."
I completed my smile
and went to the bazaar.

As I entered
the *Imam*'s wife
pulled me to the side
"Don't forget to stop by the *masjid*'s table,
and sign up for the sisters' class
about motherhood, marriage and *proper* modesty."
she wasn't finished—
pensively,
"Andmyhusbandnoticedyouandaskedmetoremindyou . . .
Weareselling MODESTLY COLORED JILBABS AND KHIMARS
Because frankly dear,
Purple is a bit Provocative."
I grinned
and calmly
took off
my lavender-purple-plum scarf
my purple sweater tunic
my perfect sandblast jeans
placed them neatly in her hands
and said . . .
"you know, you're right."

You see I figured
if they were going to treat me like a whore,
I might as well dress the part.

7 p.m.   I ain't no crooked rib

I am here.
not for your leisure or your pleasure,
nor the sole source of your poor measure in the Eyes of God.
no, I ain't no crooked rib.

not for your leisure or your pleasure
despite Islamization of a biblical fable.
no, I ain't no crooked rib,
so set your own dinner table.

despite Islamization of a biblical fable,
I am the coolness of his eye
so set your own dinner table,
place cooked morsels between my lips.

I am the coolness of his eye
creation, the product of divine Imagination.
place cooked morsels between my lips
as the Prophet's finger tips caressed Aisha's cheek.

I am simply creation, the product of divine Imagination
with my own divine directions,
the Prophet's finger tips caress Aisha's cheek
and a mind with no deficiencies, a faith that knows no bounds.

with my own divine directions
(not a *fitna* best kept locked under *khimar* and key)
and a mind with no deficiencies, a faith that knows no bounds,
I am not contingent on your existence.

not a *fitna*, best kept locked under *khimar* and key
nor the sole source of your poor measure in the Eyes of God.
I am not contingent on your existence,
I am here.

10 p.m.   Sonnet # 2

Syrupy, sappy poetry
the only way I've found to describe
dreams of this man and me
our harmony, in symphony, we vibe.

The only way I can understand
his gentleness
with the world. With my heart in hand
I rest my head on his tenderness.

The only way to illustrate
his voice—a liquid wash of sincerity
The jazzphatsmoothness of his gait
His war between intellect and humility

My heart is full of longing cries
But hope, not tears, falls from my eyes.

11:45 p.m. God-Like

A lot of people
wanna be
God-like
but i'd settle
for just knowing
God liked
me.
I know—
He loves me
but that's in the family way;
you love your sister
cause y'all come from the same womb
or home
and all that jazz
but that don't mean
you like her,
at least
not when you're 16
and she's 12.

I wanna know I
make Him happy
make Him proud;
that He speaks of me
in crowds of angels.

problem is
lately
i've forgotten that He and i
can be happy
at the same time
i've forgotten how to make that happen

i guess you could say
i've lost my way.

no.
you couldn't say that.
i know the way.
i can see it.
i was on it.

i just stopped moving.
just
            stopped
moving

i feel as though
i am
in a deep hole
with marble walls,
i can see
the world,
the way it ought to be
the way it used to,
up there.

but how do you climb marble?

i guess
you just
hafta
try.

HIJRA FROM HARLEM

Khadijah Sharif-Drinkard

I am among the strongest of faith. The Prophet Muhammad said, "Whosoever of you sees an evil action, let him change it with his hand; and if he is not able to do so, then with his tongue; and if he is not able to do so, then with his heart—and that is the weakest of faith."

I was born, the third of six children, to Muslim parents on November 19, 1971. My father was incarcerated, and my mother began her journey as a single parent, rearing her children in the housing projects of Harlem, New York. I learned early that I had to voice my opinion if I wanted to be heard. I was an innate activist and always found myself advocating on behalf of someone else and practicing my advocacy skills on my mother, whom I debated on almost every issue. I dreamed of becoming a lawyer since I was nine years old, and my life in Harlem was the training ground for my future.

I loved being a part of the Harlem community—a community mired in struggle. Despite the crackheads, prostitutes, and drug dealers, I loved my people and I had a burning desire to contribute to their advancement. My passion for Harlem stemmed from my appreciation and understanding of the historical events that took place there. I relished the fact that I was occupying a space that was once the home of such critical thinkers as Langston Hughes and James Baldwin. It was inspiring to live in a place where powerful activists like Marcus Garvey and Malcolm X led movements. It was because of people like Madam C. J. Walker and Adam Clayton Powell Jr. that our people no longer picked cotton but instead picked careers that had never been open to us before. My role models were Harriet Tubman, Sojourner Truth, Mary McCloud Bethune, Frederick Douglass, Shirley Chisolm, Barbara Jordan, and many others, especially my mother—Amidah Salahuddin, a true queen of Islam.

My mother, an activist with the NAACP in the 1960s who endured the brutal conditions of Jim Crow in the South, taught me the importance of standing up for what you believe in and taking action to effect change. While I took those lessons to heart, it was not until I read the autobiography of Shirley Chisolm that I knew I was destined for a career in public service. I was so moved by her grassroots approach to organizing that I was inspired to work on behalf of my peers. I realized that students were dropping out of school at an alarming rate, so I launched a campaign of stay-in-school rallies in the eighth grade at Adam Clayton Powell, Jr., Junior High School in Harlem. Excited to put my newly learned skills to work, I began mobilizing my peers to take action. At first people made fun of me and called me a nerd, but after the movement gained momentum, I won the respect and admiration of my peers. No matter how strong-willed I was, I still found it difficult to be publicly ridiculed. What saved me was that I believed in what I was doing. I reminded myself that I was fighting for the rights of my ancestors, many of whom were slaves and were put to death if they expressed an interest in education. It was clear to me that I had the ability to reshape how my people saw education, and perhaps the biggest challenge for me at that time was to convey that African Americans who were smart were not acting "white."

I felt blessed to be a part of a new Harlem Renaissance, where young brothers and sisters were rededicating themselves to excellence in education. It was a time of great opportunity for me, and the fact that I was being raised on welfare did not dissuade me from pursuing my dreams. From as far back as I can remember, I loved learning and despised missing school. As I walked to high school at 6:30 A.M. for advanced placement courses, I passed drug users who cheered me on, asking me to stay in school and to make something of myself so that I could make them and the rest of Harlem proud. Some of them were adults; others were my age. They had often frightened me in the alleyway, but now they were my inspiration to achieve. I guess in some ways they were also my role models—meaning they showed me what not to do in order to be successful. They had inspired me so much that at least once a week I would stay up throughout the night and study until it was time to go to school, to make up for those who were not fulfilling their potential. By taking my academic goals seriously I knew that I could shape my own destiny.

I became a true activist in high school after reading the history of former slaves like Harriet Tubman. She was my favorite role model and the one I wanted to emulate the most. So when an opportunity arose that would allow me to be a youth advisor to David N. Dinkins, then the Manhattan Borough president, I thought about what she would do and stepped out there on faith. I was one of thousands of youths applying for one of the thirty-five seats on his youth advisory committee. Nevertheless, I submitted my application and later learned I had been accepted. It meant so much to me to be accepted because, as I suspected during the application process, if I was selected I would probably be the only Muslim on the committee. My notions were confirmed at our first meeting. The committee was largely made up of middle-class youths from the best high schools and prep schools in the borough, most of whom were unfamiliar with the issues facing young people in the hood. So, the way I saw it, I had a double mission—to educate them about issues affecting impoverished youth, and to give the Muslim American a human face. The latter task was no small feat considering that it was not commonplace to see positive images of Muslims in the mainstream. Nor were there Muslims in the upper echelons of politics. My entrée into the political field as an adolescent was in fact a stance on behalf of Muslim Americans. In addition, I was an African American Muslim, no longer in the Nation of Islam, and many of my colleagues did not know that African American Muslims existed outside of the Nation of Islam.

As a committee member at the age of fifteen, I was responsible for developing viable solutions to address some of the issues that plagued New York City youth—issues such as drug dependency, teenage pregnancy/parenthood, juvenile delinquency, and gang violence. The administration thought they could learn from young people how best to serve young people. Because we were so diverse in experience and thought, we disagreed on how to achieve our goals, and that is where I first learned about collaboration. It was no small task to allow a group of ninth through twelfth graders to govern themselves and produce results; yet we had many successes. One of my proudest moments on the committee was when I testified on the topic of education reform in front of the New York City Board of Education. My experience on the committee taught me how to work with people from different ethnicities and nationalities, distinct social and economic groups, and divergent political and religious beliefs. It was a crash course in inclusiveness and tolerance, and I've used those skills of governance throughout my life.

Throughout high school I remained involved in community service activities. I served as the president of my high school's chapter of ARISTA—the National Honor Society. The mantra of the association was scholarship and service, and since my colleagues and I had the grades, our challenge was to ensure that we were of service. To that end, we led walk-a-thons and raised thousands of dollars for New York City's homeless population. We served food in soup kitchens around the city, and within our high school we volunteered as peer tutors to help our classmates with everything from calculus to physics. During my years at A. Philip Randolph Campus High School, I received a variety of awards and scholarships from many organizations and universities for academic and community service achievements. The one scholarship that I did not get was the Empire State Scholarship, which was awarded to individuals who scored above the 90th percentile on the Scholastic Aptitude Test.

In my senior year, I learned that the SAT scholarship distribution procedure had a disparate impact on women. Though women consistently have higher grade point averages than men, women tend to score lower than men on the SAT. In 1988, I joined with the American Civil Liberties Union and became the lead plaintiff in *Sharif vs. the New York State Department of Education*. After a grueling period of press conferences, interviews, and court dates, we were victorious, and the court ruled that the scholarships should have been distributed to seniors based on both their SAT scores and their GPA. In the end, I was awarded the Empire State Scholarship.

I decided to attend Columbia University, which was only nine blocks from my home in Harlem. I entered Columbia in August of 1989 as a bright-eyed and bushy-tailed seventeen-year-old ready to conquer the world. My mother and my siblings walked alongside me as I pushed my worldly possessions in a shopping cart up Broadway to the Columbia University dorms. My cart held items like my black-and-white television set with a wire coat hanger stuck in the hole where the antenna used to be, a suitcase with the few clothes that I had, a dictionary, a thesaurus, and of course, my Holy Qur'an. The latter would serve as my lifeline throughout college.

During my college tenure, serving as an activist was almost as important as my studies. I continued to work on behalf of those who were less fortunate. Because I did well academically and worked to effect change, the Muslim American Society named me Muslim Youth of the Year in 1990. I received this recognition because I had committed myself to serving all of humanity. It has always been my philosophy that Muslims should not just serve Muslims—they should be useful to society. I never focused my attention on becoming a Muslim activist; I focused my energies on being an activist, knowing that through my efforts I would inevitably serve Muslims.

The Youth of the Year award spurred me to work even harder. I joined the militant and outspoken Black Students' Organization (and I later served as its vice president). Somewhat frequently, I participated in protests against the university in an attempt to shed light on the lack of representation of people of color on the faculty and on the failure to create an African Studies Department (which was later established, in part, because of our demands). As active as I was on campus, I felt that my greatest contributions were made outside of the Victorian gates of Columbia University. On August 19, 1991, violence erupted in the Crown Heights section of Brooklyn following the death of Gavin Cato, a young Caribbean boy who was struck by a Hasidic driver as he rode his bike. In retaliation for his death, it was alleged, members of the Crown Heights community killed Yankel Rosenbaum, an Israeli student studying in the United States. For years Hasidim and West Indians had lived side-by-side in relative peace despite their distinct cultural and lifestyle differences, but all of that was about to change.

The violence was so intense that Mayor David N. Dinkins enlisted the help of community leaders and activists to serve as peacekeepers. I volunteered and was immediately deputized, which meant that I received a pass card which allowed me to identify myself as a temporary officer acting on behalf of the city and to travel freely throughout the embattled community. Mainly I calmed hysterical and angry citizens and asked them to return to their homes prior to dusk when the curfew went into effect. Some days later the violence ended but the community and the city were forever changed.

As difficult as that year was, it ended on a high note. In November 1991, Mayor Dinkins selected me and two other youths who served as peacekeepers during the Crown Heights riots to travel to South Africa and Italy as members of his delegation that included municipal officials, business executives, and education experts. I remembered the recurring dream in my head as I gazed out of my sixth floor bedroom window in the projects when I was a child. I prayed to Allah that He bless me to visit South Africa one day. At that time it seemed like an impossible dream, so far removed from my reality, since we had barely enough food to eat, made clothes from old curtains, and could hardly afford to buy items like toothpaste and deodorant. Nonetheless, I dreamed that I would return to the motherland one day, but I had no idea it would be as the guest of Nelson and Winnie Mandela.

The moment I stepped off of the plane Nelson Mandela greeted me in his usual charming and proper manner and said how happy he was that I had come home. He stated that I was so young to be a part of this historic delegation, and in return, I expressed how honored I was to be of service. It was an amazing feeling to return home where so many of my ancestors had accepted the religion of Islam. For me, the connection was more than the Afrocentricity that I shared with South Africans, it was also about the spiritual bond. When my foreparents were forced into slavery, they were compelled to relinquish their language, customs, mores, and religion. They tried to preserve the latter—practicing Islam in secret; even so, many were forced to embrace Christianity as a faith. My return home as a Muslim was a reclamation of faith and an affirmation of my ancestry.

My task on the delegation was to serve on the education committee, where I would work with students who were a part of the African National Congress youth division on developing ideas around home-schooling and freedom schools. In addition, we presented more than ten thousand books and various school supplies to Black South African students from the City of New York. The delegation traveled to Johannesburg, Pretoria, Soweto, Cape Town, and more to speak directly with citizens about how they were affected under the apartheid regime. We attended pep rallies, protests, and vigils in an effort to speak out against the inequality, injustice, and lack of due process under the law for Blacks. I remember attending one rally in a remote location of the country where we marched into the streets chanting *Amandla*

—*Nguwathu* (Power to the People). We danced the *toyi-toyi* (the South African national dance) from one shantytown to another. Being a human rights activist, I was concerned with the civil rights abuses taking place at home in Harlem, and I was equally concerned with the brutality that existed in South Africa. Apartheid was a modern form of slavery and disenfranchisement, and I was determined to leave my mark on what appeared to be the epicenter of the human rights struggle. To my surprise, however, my South African comrades left an indelible impression upon me. They endured physical abuse, mental torture, and constant humiliation. Although they were looking for answers from me, they were my inspiration.

When I returned from my trip I was more grateful than ever for our apartment in Harlem. I was thankful to have hot running water most of the time, heat after October 15th, and a welfare system that provided food stamps, which lasted until the middle of the month. My friends back home in the motherland possessed none of these conveniences and still managed to go to school, lead movements, and excel in the face of insurmountable odds. I was humbled and incredibly appreciative to Allah for His favors upon me. I also knew that despite the fact that I was doing good work, I could do more. As a result, I promised myself that I would use the information and knowledge that I had gained to educate people back home about the true circumstances of the South African people. I so desperately wanted to make Harriet Tubman proud of me. I wanted her to know that her story had touched me and that I would show my appreciation for her struggle by struggling to help those who were disenfranchised.

I prayed to Allah to continue to use me as a vehicle for change. A few months after my return from South Africa, I learned of an opportunity to serve on another delegation abroad—this time in Russia. The United Nations and Legacy International were looking for twelve youth ambassadors from around the United States to travel to Russia to study the political, economic, social, cultural, and environmental issues affecting a regime that had recently become a democracy. After a grueling application process I learned that I had been selected. I was off on another mission that would forever change me.

The delegation arrived in Moscow in the summer of 1992. We lived in the countryside and in major cities like St. Petersburg, and what struck me the most was that the people of Russia were much like the citizens of South Africa. During my stay, I visited Chernobyl and learned about nuclear power, studied the Russian language, and became a student of their culture. I also studied their religious traditions, or the lack thereof, since during Communist rule the populace was prohibited from participating in religious worship. We visited at least two dozen churches that had just reopened after the fall of Communism and witnessed the destruction that had taken place. While it is no secret that many people were Christians in Russia prior to the rise of the Communist regime, I knew that there were Muslims there as well. I requested that we incorporate a visit to a mosque into our tour and curriculum. To my surprise our guides said that they were not aware of any. I was determined to visit a mosque, and so on the penultimate day of our journey I found a mosque in the city of St. Petersburg. It was indeed a relic, but a beautiful one that was undergoing a much-needed facelift. Nevertheless, you could see its beauty and history in each stone that was laid. I felt complete at that point because I had linked a piece of Russian history to my experience.

It meant a great deal for me to connect a piece of their history with my own life experiences. To see the evidence that Muslims had not only existed in Russia but had flourished there was amazing. I realized that Muslims penetrated every corner of the earth.

When I returned from Russia the youth ambassadors toured the United States, reporting on how this new democracy was being forged abroad. The trip was a rare opportunity to witness the embryonic stages of a democracy, and we eagerly presented our findings to community organizations and universities.

★ ★ ★ ★

Two years later, I achieved my childhood dream and began my legal studies at Fordham University School of Law. During my law school tenure I enjoyed my coursework as well as extracurricular activities such as serving as the National Parliamentarian for the National Black Law Students Association (NBLSA). Being affiliated with NBLSA provided me with the opportunity to travel around the country for regional meetings, participate in conferences, and preside over the annual national convention. I served in that capacity for just one year because I had my sights set on yet another delegation abroad—this time in China.

In 1995, I was informed that the United Nations was holding its Fourth World Conference on Women, and this time it would take place in Beijing. Although I was not a member of a nongovernmental organization, nor did I have any affiliation with the United Nations, I was determined to participate in this conference to represent the concerns of Muslim American women. As a result, I attended an orientation meeting at the United Nations for people who were traveling to China. At the meeting, I learned that because I had been a journalist for the *Muslim Journal* for the previous six years I would have special access as a member of the press corps. Not only would I be able to cover the conference, but I would be able to participate on the committees as a representative of the Muslim American Society. I was prepared in all respects, and thanks to the help of just a few generous individuals, I raised enough money to cover all of my expenses for the entire three weeks that I stayed in Beijing.

While in Beijing and in the remote location of Huairo, where most of the conference was held, I met the most amazing women from around the world, including many I was familiar with, like Winnie Mandela and the widow of Malcolm X, Dr. Betty Shabazz (we became friendly while serving together on the South African delegation). I participated in protests to end the trafficking of slave girls in Nepal and India, and I met with Muslim women from Iran who had been persecuted because they were scholars. I sat on the Document Committee for the Women of Color Caucus and assisted in drafting the Platform for Action—the document that was born from the conference detailing the international rights of women. I was moved by the stories of women struggling in every part of the world, and I was inspired to be a better woman because of it. Perhaps my greatest task there was to ensure that people knew that Islam had already bestowed God-given rights on women and that no document could recreate the rights that had already been provided to us by Allah. While I went there to share information, I certainly had no idea that I would spend as much time as I did propagating the religion of Islam in an effort to reveal the balance, justice, and freedom inherent to our way of life. Upon my return I shared the information with the Muslim American community as I traveled the country, lecturing about the conference and on the importance of African American Muslims having a stake in the process of going forward.

As I looked back on this experience over the years, it reminded me of being on a mini-hajj. When I went to Mecca in 2001 to complete my rites as a Muslim, I remembered that in China, like on hajj, there were people from all over the world coming together for one purpose. On hajj our goal was to bear witness to the Oneness of Allah (the Most High), and in China we were there to stand up for the rights of women.

The conference reminded me of how fortunate I am to practice Islam in America, where women could pursue education, serve as elected officials, walk freely in the streets or eat in restaurants without their husbands, and drive cars. It was there that I truly began to appreciate being an American Muslim. The countries with the worst records on women's rights were often led by Muslim governments. My participation in the conference and my trip to China gave me a better appreciation for the United States of America.

Two years later I graduated from law school, and many people, including myself, thought that I was headed for a career in public service. However, I took a job in a training program at MTV Networks that would teach me how to become an entertainment lawyer. A year and three months after starting that program, I became the first lawyer hired at Nickelodeon as in-house counsel that had evaded the brutal clutches of law-firm life.

Despite my newfound interest in entertainment law, I still felt incomplete without participating in the political arena. As a result, I decided to work on the presidential campaign for Bill Bradley. While Senator Bradley's senior staff members wooed me to join the campaign full-time, I opted to stick with the Nickelodeon position and to volunteer my services instead. As a volunteer I campaigned in Vermont, worked the Iowa caucuses, and helped create a letter-writing campaign for Women in Support of Bill Bradley. My appetite for politics had been whetted again, and soon afterward I threw my hat into the ring and became the first Muslim to seek public office in the Township of Maplewood, New Jersey.

When I decided to run for the Township Committee (the equivalent of the city council), there were only ten weeks until the primary in June of 2002. Some well-intentioned people who were members of the Committee convinced me that I would be a good choice. I had never run for public office before, and I had only lived in my town for a year and a half. I had a lot to learn about Maplewood, and I had to know it before the debate against our opponents. My running mate and I walked the streets every night, knocking on the doors of residents to explain why we wanted them to vote for us. We held coffees in people's homes setting forth our agenda, answered questions about our solutions for decreasing property taxes, educational reform, and environmental issues, and attended every major public hearing that was held. In the end we lost by three hundred votes in the primary, but I received the highest number of votes in six districts, which meant that I won the second highest number of districts in the race. Ironically, the gentleman who won the least number of districts actually won the primary because his running mate carried him. I learned a lot about politics from working on campaigns and serving as an advisor to political officials, but I learned the most from actually running for office myself. It was perhaps one of the scariest things that I have ever done because I was putting the world on notice that I wanted my voice to be heard.

I was also curious to see how people would respond to me, since my name was clearly a Muslim name and we reside in a pretty uppity town despite its sprinkled diversity. What I found from that experience is that some people harbor prejudice, but most constituents are willing to hear your agenda and to see if you have viable solutions to their problems, and that is all one can ask. I am certain that one day I will run for public office again and that I will win.

My dream is to become the first Muslim president of the United States. I have had this goal since high school and believe that one day it will be a reality. As a Muslim president, I would strive to be a modern-day example of how Prophet Muhammad governed—respecting and valuing the contributions of all people. When I become president it will be a different world. Islam will no longer be seen as a threat to the West. The world will have a more in-depth understanding of the contributions of Islam and Muslims. We as Muslims will no longer allow others, who claim to practice our religion, to highjack our glorious way of life. Both Muslims and friends of our faith will have made monumental strides toward understanding our own roles in reshaping the world and our place in it. I believe that a Muslim president is needed to bring about balance, justice, and true freedom for all people.

I see running for office as a task that is as important as completing school and voting. Despite not winning a seat I am busier than ever. After the election many people called upon me to serve on a variety of boards. I could not accept all of the invitations that were extended to me, so I was extremely selective. Today I serve as a member of the Planning Board overseeing planning and development issues for the Township of Maplewood. In addition, I am currently an executive committee member of my neighborhood association, where my primary responsibility is handling the concerns of community residents. My involvement in community issues goes back to my roots when I served as the first female vice chairperson of the board of directors for The Valley, Inc.—the Harlem-based nonprofit organization where I was once a participant and a founding member of the women's empowerment group called the Circle of Sistahs. My faith and activism has allowed me to effect change carrying picket signs in the streets, making decisions in the boardroom, and coordinating book club discussions where we deal with hot topics around religion and race. I have found several methods as effective vehicles for change—the key is to be open and flexible to them all.

When I first became dedicated to public service I was inspired to make a change because I knew that we deserved better. I knew that my ancestors had struggled so much for the freedoms that I enjoyed, and I wanted to repay the debt. While today I feel similarly, I also know that being a mother of a young daughter has increased my desire to make this world a better place. Whenever I think about how exhausted I am after work as I head off to my next meeting after dinner, I remember that my little girl is counting on me to reshape our society so that she may have a better chance at succeeding than I had. Just when I feel that I need to quit a committee because I have to leave my house at dawn in order to attend a meeting, I am reminded that without sacrifice there is no progress. As I reflect back on all that I have accomplished, I believe that my greatest achievement was giving birth to Jalsa. It was through giving birth that I began to understand the true meaning of service. I pray that one day I can be her Harriet Tubman. I want to inspire her so that she understands and appreciates her power. If I can be as good a mother to Jalsa as my mother was to me, then we will have won. And that is the task currently at hand.

THE MUSLIM IN THE MIRROR

Mohja Kahf

"I don't care if I never see another Muslim for as long as I live."
That thought became a refrain in my mind somewhere around
1998. Fine, I amended, except the one I sleep with. He can stay.
And my children. Parents. Five brothers, a sister. In-laws, I guess.
Several best friends.

Oh, yeah, and the Muslim in the mirror: Myself.

But I didn't want to hear another word of Islam-talk for as long
as I live. Islam is a way of life this. Islamic identity that. Sunni
this, Shi'a that. Dawah this, shari'a that. Conservative Muslims.
Muslim feminists. Liberal Muslims. Nation Muslims. Ahmediya.
Wahhabiya. Sufis. Traditionals. Orthodox. Arab-hating Muslims
and racist Arab Muslims. Converts and "reverts." Political Islam.
From radical revolutionaries to flag-waving Republican Muslims. Palestine, Kashmir, and the latest Muslim cause *du jour.*
Hijab yes, hijab no, hijab maybe. Sister do, sister don't. When "sister" means the brother wants me to toe the line, then I ain't your
sister, mister.

I was sick of the scene. And of the God that went with the
Islam-talk. God and the Prophet. Do it for the sake of God. For
the pleasure of God. For obeying God. All that glib talk of God.
All my life I've heard it.

I was fed up with Islam-talk. There are other things in life be-
sides the religion game, you know. Good things. Beautiful things.
I discovered that it is entirely possible to ditch the Islam-scene and

still seek God. It is possible that all that busy religion work was what was keeping me from spirituality.

Oh, I was still a Muslim. No one was gonna take that away from me. Especially not the anti-Muslim bigots. If there's anyone I was more sick and tired of than Muslims, it's Muslim-bashers. No one is allowed to criticize Islam and Muslims but those who do it from love. Those who do it from hate, step aside. And step aside, those who do it as a way to fame and fortune funded by neo-conservatives who think they can *kaCHING* up genuine "reform" in Islam and manufacture docile little McMuslims for the maintenance of U.S. McHegemony in the world. Neocons can kiss my Islamic ass.

Neither will I swerve away from forthrightly criticizing my beloved faith community because such criticism is seen as aiding and abetting the bigots who are vying to close our charities, to criminalize our beliefs and practices and even our Arabic script, and to isolate us inside a barbed wire of hate. I will not circle my wagons around the mosque, will not yield in fearful worry to the entreaties of the wagon-circlers inside nor to the shouts of the hatemongers outside. I function within this double bind. I strategize around it with every move I make, every piece I write.

Back at that moment when I said "I've had it with Islam-talk," even then I still acknowledged the wisdom and beauty in the tradition. I rejoiced in it. I just didn't want all the other crap that comes with it in many contemporary Islamic worldviews. I was tired of butting my head up against an Islam-brickwall that would not move.

Why I need a migraine every Friday after the *khutba* (that is, when I was in places that allowed me to attend *juma*; my local mosque until recently had little space or welcome for women at *juma*, and now that the new mosque is built women can pray *juma* only on a mezzanine with opaque fiberglass cutting off all visual contact with the main hall). I was tired of feeling isolated in the Islamic conversation. I had years ago left the conservative worldview and hung with the liberal modernist Muslims, who emphasize the flexibility and versatility of Islamic laws and traditions, but that didn't help for long. In the end the liberals were still inside the box, as far as I could tell, unable to think outside the forms into which Islam had rigidified over the centuries. Something more radical was needed. Not to dump all of tradition, but to take the best strands of it and create Islam afresh for a new generation.

Maybe I was crazy. No one else I knew seemed to want to do that, and by myself, I didn't know how. Well, okay, not "no one"; there were a few scattered individuals here and there who had similar thoughts. But maybe they were as crazy as I was. The fight took too much high logic for my brain to handle. Too much sadness for my tired heart. I dropped out. I would rather have new ground to explore. Culture, art, music, poetry. Not polemics but beauty. Wherever you turn, there is the Face of God. So let me come at life a different way for a while.

It was the summer of 2001. I got a phone call. Decided to try a little volunteering. Not for Islam, but for humanity at large. Do some service in the world. The women's shelter called me, needing a translator for a beaten woman. Muslim, the religious kind. Scared, the battered woman kind. I went. Better me than some Muslim who'd try to send her back to him, saying, "Sister mustn't stay with these kaffir kind, in the home is where you belong." Better me than some non-Muslim trying to help her while believing that her religion was the problem and if she'd only dump it, take that veil off her head, and follow a Western model, she'd be suddenly liberated. That would only send a very traditional woman, attached to her religious symbols, recoiling right back into the arms of the batterer.

I found out that beaten women horrify me. Their abjection, their defeatedness, reminded me of something inside me, something cringing and afraid and weak. I know that the battered woman has an altered sense of reality in which he is all-powerful, that she can't help her schizoid dance of "I want to live—but I'm going to return and live abjectly under his raised arm. I don't want to die—but I won't take strong steps to protect my life." But she can. She can help herself. It's the voice inside that won't let her, the voice of the man-pleasing woman she thinks she has to be.

This particular woman's man-pleasing and self-killing voice implicated Islam. Oh, there was no dancing out of this one with the neat steps of Islamic apologetics, like the stuff I was raised on, the stuff I learned to spout as a youth: "Islam gave women their rights fourteen hundred years ago." Nor was the sellout speech of the Muslim woman I used to be, lauded for her Islamic knowledge, any help: "It's just that Muslim women aren't educated about their rights." Blame Muslim women for not being educated about their rights? No, not the women alone—blame the *ulema*, the Islamic activists and preachers, the mosque communities, along with the women for not educating themselves with a consciousness of their inner liberation in God, and for instead inculcating in women, day in, day out, that an ethic of wifely submission to male authority is godly. Blame ourselves for perpetuating and defending a sexist set of assumptions we keep calling Islam. Blame our Muslim American leaders for running our mosques and organizations like "men's clubs" (in the words of Dr. Ingrid Mattson, vice president of the Islamic Society of North America, in an interview with Asra Nomani). Blame the masses of our community members for passively accepting this Muslim sexism. Blame them for trying to silence women and men who try to change this, by mistrusting their motives, mocking them, and casting doubt on their faith.

And don't even try "It's not Islam, it's just culture." Our sexism is embedded in Islam itself. Because Islam is not just some pie-in-the-sky ideal, but what people practice as Islam and what the scholars preach as Islam. They are reality and we deal with them daily as Islam. If you think such a thing as "pure Islam" existed, even for five minutes in C.E. 623, think again. Islam is always manifested inside a particular culture and in specific, earth-rooted human bodies, and our job now is to birth a new Islam, a new Islamic culture. This Islam-on-the-ground-as-a-lived-reality needs to step up and take credit for the specific ways in which it oppresses women as well as the ways in which it liberated women fourteen hundred years ago.

This woman at the shelter sincerely believed that Islam required of her submission to a man who was regularly beating her black-and-blue, burning her with hot iron instruments, strangling her with his hands. When I saw her worldview and how Islam figured in it, I was outraged, horrified, disgusted. She actually believed she deserved the beatings because she had defied orders of her husband. She felt herself deeply, profoundly, to be the one in the wrong, and she felt she'd multiplied the wrong by leaving the house. A disobedient woman deserves chastisement, right? Never mind that she disobeyed him from an instinct for survival that—thank God—had not been totally killed in her by Islam, by her Islam-inculcated, Muslim-community-supported belief in wifely obedience.

What kind of a horrible God did she believe in, I asked myself, who would let her be trapped like this, in a death-in-life, without letting her believe in a means of escape? What kind of horrible God did we—Muslims—believe in to allow any number of women to go around with this idea in their heads, that they are supposed to live these lives of abject subordination in order to be good Muslim women?

The shelter case may be a pathological example of how Islam manifested in one woman's life. There are kinder, gentler faces of patriarchal Islam. But it took an extreme case to shock me out of my paralysis about participating in the modern Islamic conversation. Because the internalized vision of Islam this woman had is one of the faces of Islam that we have allowed to evolve and exist and thrive. For it is not just this one woman who believes in this hopelessly inegalitarian version of Islam, it is many, and we are all implicated. For our cowardice. For not fighting the ethic of wifely submission in Islamic discourses. For not rescuing the compassionate and pro-woman face of Islam.

Victims of the pre-Islamic Arab custom of female infanticide were traditionally murdered by burial alive. They were rescued by the Qur'an in the seventh century, rescued by a vision of social change that addressed their human rights in a bold, emphatic way never before thought of in that society. We have allowed the bodies of women to become the sacrificial victims again. And we have allowed the feminine body of Islam to be buried alive in the sand, over and over again.

We are implicated for dropping out of the community and its discourses when we are alienated. For giving up on changing Islam. Like I had. For giving up on being part of the conversation, the Islam-talk. Instead of staying and rolling up our sleeves and working for reform, even though it may mean a weekly headache and getting splattered by the mudslingers in personal attacks on our Islamic legitimacy, our moral character, our right to have a say in the Muslim community, and our faith.

Why I need this Islam-talk? Because it was the only talk that would get this battered woman out of her old worldview. She would not leave without Islam. She had to take Islam with her to make a new life, a new way of thinking about life as a woman alone in the world. I had to give her a jolt of Islam-CPR, and I needed it myself, too.

To help the woman back at the shelter, I had to go back into the forest of liberal Islam and seek the Muslim feminists with whom I had lost patience because their work was too slow and piecemeal for me. They worked within existing Islamic paradigms but tried to craft a more woman-affirming manifestation of the laws. I dug out my old dog-eared copies of Dr. Rifaat Hassan and Dr. Amina Wadud to arm the woman with Qur'anic concepts so as to refute the abject woman she thought she had to be with other concepts firmly rooted in Islam. I looked up things on the website of the Muslim Women's League. I called up my ever-helpful and enduring best friend Dr. Asifa Quraishi, an Islamic law expert, to get some answers.

But it was not only liberal Islam that helped me with the woman at the shelter. I sought aid from conservative Islam, too. Look, conservative Muslims do not want wives to get pummeled any more than progressives, okay? The conservative Muslim vision, despite its inegalitarian views of gender, is not ultimately one of a home devoid of safety and dignity for women, after all. I called up the imam of a major Midwestern mosque. As soon as he saw the police report of the beating, he wrote up an Islamic divorce for the woman from the man she thought she couldn't divorce Islamically.

The battered woman did not know that she had the Islamic right to leave her husband unilaterally because of *darrar,* harm that he inflicted on her. I knew that she did have this right, had spent many years of my life pursuing these concepts and rights, and could tell her all about them, but she would not take these Islamic concepts from me and act on them, because she, being a traditional woman, had to hear it from a man. A man with a beard who looked to her like an Islamic authority. Thank God for the supportive conservative Muslim men—even the ones who parse the meaning of the "beat verse" by saying, "Yes, but he can only beat her with a handkerchief," which is still too conservative for me. But if the alternative is this traditional Muslim woman thinking her husband had the right to beat her unconditionally, I'll take it, and pass it to her happily, as a first step anyway. I called upon my conservative Muslim family. My father, an Islamic economics scholar, gave me a review of the woman's rights according to Islamic law and helped me brush up on empowering Islamic concepts to pass on to her. The rest of my family—mother, uncles, aunts, brothers—sent money for her and gave me moral support and encouragement.

And it worked. I could see her latch on to the concepts, which were new to her but whose grounding in Qur'anic values she immediately recognized with a deep *yaqin*-certainty. I actually watched her gird herself around with them and fend off the well-meaning mosque community members, the next time they came at her with "A wife leaving the husband's house to spend the night outside with strangers is un-Islamic, a disgrace!" Now she could say, "Tell you what the un-Islamic disgrace is, it is his beating me nearly to death, because *darrar* is not allowed in Islam, and shari'a is there to protect five things, and one of them is life, physical well-being. My physical well-being is as important to God as husbandly authority. And I am not with strangers, I am in a place where they have provided me with a Muslim woman with Islamic answers. She brought me a Qur'an and a prayer rug the very first night. So how can this be such a den of iniquity and immorality and a compromise to my family's honor?" And if the local Muslim people said to her, "You can't get divorced Islamically unless he grants it!" she now responded, "Yes I can, I can initiate unilateral divorce through a judge, or I can get *khul*. How could you think God would not legislate a way out for me in this deadly situation? That would not be just or merciful, and God is just and Rahman."

Even though I reentered contemporary Muslim discourse by seeking old allies among conservative and liberal Muslims, I could not stay in their modes of thinking about Islam. More daring Muslim thought had been going on for years, but my ears had not been equipped to pick it up. Now I had new antennae, and I tuned in. I didn't feel isolated anymore: Everywhere I turned, the faces of freethinking Muslims and alternative Islamic discourses —from other periods of Islamic history as well as in today's world—were becoming visible to me. Even many Muslim figures I had formerly encountered as conservative or liberal were themselves shifting in their orientation. For example, I discovered that Amina Wadud had already moved past the borderlands of liberal Islamic discourse and was moving deeply into what we now seem to be calling the progressive part of the Islamic spectrum. For another example, Sufi discourse, whose deeply traditional, hierarchical side I had known for years, now showed me its other face through members of the Jerrahi order and of the Bawa Muhaiyaddeen Fellowship, a Sufism that still respected tradition but was far more fluid and open in its form.

Finally, with the help of friends and guides on the path, I began to free myself of the false god who lived within, the god whose obsession is obedience. I had been battered by an internalized idea of this god. My prior clumsy attempts to make my way around him by myself gave me that crazy schizoid feeling—that

I must be doing something terribly wrong in going outside the house of tradition, disobeying, while a *yaqin*-certainty told me that *not* to do so violated everything I knew to be sacred.

Grateful for the guidance that had come my way, I began to seek al-Rahman, the Divine whose countenance is compassion, loving kindness, mercy: Rahma. A word which comes from the Arabic root *rahm*: the womb. I began to seek the womanly body of Islamic discourse, to pull her out of the sand in which she has been half-buried and struggling for a long, long time. The distressed woman I was sent to help was myself in another form, an abject form my selfhood has taken sometimes, a cringing woman inside me that I tried to forget. She straightened up, uncringed. I am back. I am back and kicking.

BEING THE LEADER I WANT TO SEE IN THE WORLD

Asra Q. Nomani

MORGANTOWN, W.V.—My list of accomplishments was long in the Morgantown High yearbook for the class of 1982. But I was always the secretary, never the president.

Somehow I wasn't able to catapult ahead of Kaye Ingle to be president of Math Honor. Coach Becky Rice named me the Most Improved Player on our volleyball squad, but Lynette White won honors as the captain and the Most Valuable Player. In track, I was used to third place, but never first place. It was only at the *Red and Blue Journal* that I was a leader as the editor in chief, but even then only a faithful staff of one, Leslie Propst, seemed to listen to my instructions while the rest went their own way.

For so much of my life I was self-motivating, ambitious, and hard-working, but, formally, I sought the quality of leadership outside myself, never within. During college, I became a journalist and dutifully recorded and reflected upon the events around me. I was the observer but never the one on stage. I became a staff reporter at the *Wall Street Journal* at the age of twenty-three, but I never raised my hand to go on the management track to become an editor. I never thought I was worthy. I broke stories about alleged price fixing by the airline industry, leading to a Justice Department investigation and multimillion dollar settlement. I challenged the management decisions of corporate titans. And I uncovered the fraudulent business practices of a young airline industry scam artist, sending him to jail. By the standards of media analysis, I was a gatekeeper, but I was never an opinion leader.

Only through a traumatic sequence of events in my life was I able to understand clearly an essential truth to living life to the fullest: The leadership we so often seek from outside ourselves, from titles or popularity, can best be found from within. Leadership often emerges at times of crisis when we are faced with critical and fateful choices. It was my time of crisis that led me to decide that as a Muslim woman I could no longer be just an observer in the struggle for the rights of women in my religion. The man who led my native country of India to liberation from colonial rule, Mahatma Gandhi, has inspired many with his words, "You must be the change you wish to see in the world." What I learned is that this is true of leadership: There will come a time in each of our lives when we must make the difficult choice to stop seeking leadership from others and assert it ourselves. What we will discover is that our entire lives had been leading us to that moment. We must be the leader we wish to see in the world.

My awakening started in the most unlikely of places: a bungalow in an upper-class neighborhood of Karachi, Pakistan. After a band of Muslim men hijacked planes and crashed them into the World Trade Center on September 11, 2001, in the name of Islam, I jetted to Pakistan as a journalist for *Salon* magazine, hoping to build some understanding between the Muslim world and the West. Unexpectedly, I fell in love with a charming Pakistani-Muslim man, and I rented a bungalow to pursue the romance and finish a book I was writing on leave from the *Wall Street Journal*. On January 23, 2002, a dear friend and colleague from the *Journal* visited me. His name was Daniel Pearl. He and his wife, Mariane, were living in Bombay, where Danny was stationed as the *Journal*'s South Asia bureau chief. The next day, as a family of parrots swooped overhead in the bright Karachi sky, Mariane and I waved goodbye to Danny as he slipped into a yellow taxi to go to an interview. We expected him back for dinner that night, but he didn't return. As night slipped into morning, I sat in front of Danny's Toshiba laptop with Mariane and began a desperate search to find my friend. Three days later, we learned the secret behind Danny's disappearance. A cadre of men had kidnapped him in the name of Islam, and, embracing an ideology of hatred toward Jews, they rationalized their kidnapping because Danny was Jewish. Pakistani intelligence officers endangered my safety by fingering me, erroneously, as a spy for India. They paid my boyfriend a visit, and he arrived at my house. "My parents don't want me to see you anymore," he told me.

I was stunned. He was abandoning us. I cried, "But you have a choice."

"I've made my choice," he said, firmly.

"No!" I wept.

He turned and walked away, and I descended into a walk-in closet that I had used for moments of solitude. I wept alone, my body shaking from my sense of aloneness, and then, wiping my tears with the back of my hand, I emerged to return to my computer. I had made my own choice. I would continue to try to find Danny. To me, loyalty superseded fear. At that moment, I knew that I could not look for leadership in Pakistani law enforcement, the U.S. State Department, or the FBI, let alone in my boyfriend. I had to rise to the occasion to help guide this investigation. Mariane and I turned my home into the headquarters for the search to find Danny, with law enforcement people streaming through at all hours. My dining room table was the command center.

In the fourth week of trying to find Danny, I faced a second test of my character. I discovered that I was pregnant. I did not know what to do. My pregnancy was a crime according to the strictest interpretation of shari'a, or Islamic law, in Pakistan, punishable by a hundred lashes because I was unwed. I called my boyfriend to my house and told him the news. "I have to go," he told me. I was shocked. I pled for direction from him. Instead, he walked away again. Over the next several days, he told me he did not want to keep the baby. In torment, a week later, I and the world learned that Danny had been murdered and beheaded.

Shattered, I left Pakistan, deeply conflicted about the life within me. Over the next months, my boyfriend told me he would accept the baby and be with me. I kept looking to him for leadership in the family we had created. He broke promises to see me and failed to arrive for my baby's birth in Morgantown on October 16, 2002. A few weeks later, my baby beside me, I called my boyfriend in the quiet of the night. In the dark, I accidentally dialed 911. When the dispatcher for the West Virginia State Police answered, I hung up the phone. The phone rang. It was the dispatcher, inquiring about the call. "Is everything okay?" I said I had made a mistake. "Is someone holding a gun to your head?" she asked.

At that moment, I realized that someone was in fact holding a gun to my head, and she was me. I was looking for leadership in my boyfriend for the family that was my son and me. It dawned on me that, as a mother, I had to be a leader to my son. I was the CEO of my family, and I could not wait for another. That awakening led me to another door, one that had long been closed to me and millions of other women around the world.

As a leader for my son, responsible for his education as a Muslim, I walked up to the front door of my new mosque in Morgantown on the eve of Ramadan 2003. It was the opening night for the mosque, which my father had helped build as a founder of our local Muslim community and member of the board of trustees. A shocking thing happened. The president of the board, a retired professional from our local West Virginia University, yelled at me: "Sister, take the back door!" He wanted me to take a side wooden stairwell to a rear door. Stunned, I proceeded through the front door, but somehow knew that I was not allowed to go up the front stairwell. It led to a main hall forbidden to women. I went dutifully up a rear stairwell into a secluded balcony where the other women and I were expected to sit, staring at a hip-high solid wall that blocked all visual access to the prayer leader and sermons in the main hall below. For the first ten days of Ramadan, I kept returning to the balcony, angry and frustrated at the segregation of women into separate and unequal quarters. I looked around for other women similarly frustrated. They were, but none wanted to venture into the main hall. Through the study of my religion, I learned that women had an Islamic right to be in the main prayer hall without being separated by a curtain, wall, or partition. I realized that it was my responsibility to claim rights denied to me. I had to be a leader for myself and my son.

On the eleventh day of Ramadan, my mother, father, niece, and nephew went with me as I walked with my son through the front door and ascended the short stairwell into the main hall. To be a leader, I had to overcome my own fears. As long as I remained hostage to my fears, I could not blame others, culture, or religion for imprisoning me. I had to create new realities by transcending my fears. The board president again yelled at me.

"Sister! It's better for you upstairs," he said, towering over my mother and me, as we sat waiting for the dawn prayer to begin.

"Brother, I'm happy praying here," I answered.

And my mother, an inspiration to me, chided him for yelling at others in the mosque. He yelled some more about closing the mosque. But he didn't, and we completed our prayers. That night, I returned for the evening Ramadan prayers, and a horde of men surrounded me to tell me to leave. "We cannot pray if *she* is here," a man declared. I knew that wasn't true. Where were the men who also knew this to be true? I looked for them to stand up to protect me. The only man who did was my father. "She is doing nothing wrong," he told the men. The rest of the men remained silent. Still, I stood my ground because I was starting to learn that being a leader can be lonely.

The next day, in my parents' kitchen, my father told me the board of trustees had met. They had voted four to one to make the front door and main hall solely for the use of men. My father was the lone dissenting vote. "But *you* are our leaders," I protested. "You have a moment of opportunity to choose to do the right thing, but you do the *wrong* thing! How could you do that to us?"

My father shook his head in frustration. "I tried," he said. "They would not listen to me."

"You have betrayed us as leaders," I said, disillusioned.

Dismayed, I tried to turn to the board for leadership. It could still do the right thing and reverse its vote. The board president jetted out of the country after the vote. The acting board president refused all of my requests for a meeting. Each day I grew more frustrated. I realized that I had one talent, writing, that had never let me down. I called Muslim leaders around the country for their perspective about the rights of women in mosques. The replies were empowering. In New York, Daisy Khan, the executive director of the ASMA Society, an American Muslim organization, told me that, as mothers, women had a responsibility to be teachers for their children. In Hartford, Connecticut, scholar Ingrid Mattson, a vice president at the Islamic Society of North America, the largest organization of American Muslims, acknowledged to my shock that mosques were akin to "men's clubs."

And I discovered that the problem was only growing worse. A mosque report by the country's largest Muslim organizations, including ISNA and the Council on American-Islamic Relations, a civil rights group, documented the fact that two out of three mosques in the United States in 2000 required women to pray behind a curtain, wall, or partition, compared to one out of two mosques surveyed in 1994. To my horror, one in three mosques *banned* women from holding a board position. The biggest names in American Muslim leadership had spoken about this mosque report, but I could not find a single mention of this blatant and systemic discrimination. American Muslim women were subject to gender apartheid in our communities, and nobody was aggressively challenging the status quo.

As with my local mosque leadership, I felt betrayed by my national Muslim leaders. Why didn't they protect me and other women like me? Why in the 21st century were we harassed if we tried to reclaim rights Muslim women got in the 7th century? As I pondered these questions, a headline from Agence France-Presse, the French wire service, crossed my eyes: "Women in Indian Village Fed Up with Sexism, Build Own Mosque." A group of women in an Indian village, annoyed at what they considered sexist decisions made by male authorities, particularly in divorce cases, had decided to build their own mosque with its own dispute settlement body. If these women could stand up for their rights, how could I, a Muslim woman enjoying the privileges of the West, squander mine? I took my thoughts to paper and published an essay in the *Washington Post* taking a stand, as I had never done in my fifteen years as a professional journalist at the *Wall Street Journal.* "A Rebel in the Mosque: Going Where I Know I Belong," the headline read, with the image of a lone woman praying in a mosque. The image wasn't of me, but it captured how I felt on so many occasions at the mosque when I stood alone behind a phalanx of rows of up to 150 men. What had I done, taking a stand?

I sank into deep contemplation as I digested an immediate onslaught of letters I received in response to my essay in the *Washington Post.* "Keep strong and keep going!!!!" a Muslim woman community organizer wrote from San Diego, California. A Christian woman wrote her appreciation: "Your work is for everyone, not just Muslims." Sitting in my split-level 1970s prefab childhood home in Morgantown, I had somehow struck a nerve. Even I was surprised. One message particularly spoke to me because it underscored how Muslim women are today in the same situation as African Americans in the 1950s, denied rights the law didn't yet protect. Gwendolyn Zohara Simmons, an assistant professor of religion at the University of Florida in Gainesville, wrote:

"As an African American over 50, for the first 18 years of my life, I had to go into public places via back doors, enter the bus from side doors or sit in the back of the bus, or sit in balconies at theatres, or have special days to go into Museums, Zoos, etc., if I was permitted to go at all, because I am black. I went to jail, was beaten, threatened with death and other things to change this. I feel just as angry when I have to go into back doors, side doors, etc., sit in balconies or in the back in silence in the Mosques that I attend today, and that is all of them that I have ever attended (except in Mecca, ironically) since being a Muslim. It is absolutely disgraceful in my opinion that we women must go through the humiliation that Asra Nomani went through. I admire her; I salute her, and I pray that I live long enough to see the men and women of Islam stand up to the forces of repression and hatred of women and change these practices. It is long overdue!"

As with the American civil rights struggle, every nation's struggle for independence from colonial rule, and all social movements, I realized it is the personal convictions of ordinary individuals that spark revolution, reform, and rebirth. Looking for guidance, I called the Leadership Council on Civil Rights, a Washington group with leaders of the struggle for civil rights among African Americans. I examined the times of the Prophet Muhammad. When he first received revelations from God, meditating in a cave outside Mecca, he ran to his wife, Khadijah, fearful. She showed the character of a leader by remaining calm and guiding him to accept the divine messages he was receiving. Without her keen stewardship, Islam could not have been born. I studied the lives of the caliphs, or leaders, following the life of the Prophet Muhammad.

Meanwhile, the ban in Morgantown remained in place. The men turned a cold shoulder to me each time I returned to the main hall, and I felt like a rule breaker.

Where could I turn for leadership? I set my eyes on the Council on American-Islamic Relations. It pitched itself to the world as an ACLU of the Muslim world, a leader in protecting the rights of Muslims. I filed a gender discrimination complaint against my mosque. I became a case number. And the organization concluded it couldn't get involved. I turned to the Islamic Society of North America. It had started a leadership development center. Its director intervened and tried to mediate a solution. It helped in part but it didn't dismantle the engrained sexism we faced as women in our mosque.

Who could help me? I was looking so much for external solutions that I was confused when the mayor of Morgantown, a former classmate of mine at West Virginia University, Ron Justice, asked me to speak to his leadership class. "Me?" I asked.

"Yes, you," he answered.

"What could I possibly talk about?"

"Talk about your experience challenging inequities at your mosque," he said. "You're a leader. You're an agent for change." I listened to his words in amazement. I didn't believe I had the credentials to lecture even the teen presidents of fraternities and sororities about leadership. Somehow, I stood before the class and led them through the inner dialogue with which I decided to take a stand. I left, knowing something important had happened in my path toward self-realization, but not fully understanding what it was.

As women, I started to realize, we needed to stand together, with the men who supported us beside us. In the days after writing publicly about the issues of women at mosques, I was introduced to an inspiring network of powerful Muslim women. We had a dream: We would march to the mosque in Morgantown and affirm the Islamic rights of women everywhere. But could we accomplish this daunting task?

The answer came to me most unexpectedly. I went to a lecture by Eleanor Smeal, founder of the Feminist Majority, an organization created to protect women's rights. In a lecture hall in the campus of West Virginia University, she told the audience, "It doesn't take a hundred women to create a movement. It just takes five." Listening to her in the back rows, I pondered this notion, and it gave me strength. I had joined forces with Saleemah Abdul-Ghafur, a powerful woman in Atlanta whom I would have cast in "The Apprentice," Donald Trump's reality TV show aimed at spotting the next corporate leader, and Samina Ali, an author in San Francisco who had dared to write a Muslim feminist novel. We were three. We recruited to our cause Mohja Kahf, a woman I considered the Muslim world's answer to Maya Angelou, and Sarah Eltantawi, a forceful public spokeswoman on the toughest of TV talk news programs. We were five. And we had as our anchors two remarkable women: my mother, Sajida Nomani, a retired boutique owner, and Saleemah's mother, Nabeelah Abdul-Ghafur, a writer and activist. Somehow, I realized we could create our own reality and not define our lives by other people's realities. Together, we did the unthinkable. We marched in unison with the same chant traditionally exclaimed on the path to Mecca.

"At Your service, oh Lord! Here I come!"

We were arriving, each one of us, in each of our unique ways, on our own. This, I now understood, was what it meant to be a leader in our own lives. We didn't have to simply cede leadership over to another, considering ourselves unqualified. It was important for us to assume leadership in all aspects of our lives, from the spiritual to the intellectual. We challenged one of the deepest denials of women's full expression: her ability to lead prayer. In the seventh century, the Prophet had told a woman, Umm Waraqa, she could lead prayer at her house, a male slave following her. Knowing that the Qur'an does not differentiate between the morality of a free man and a slave, religious scholars such as a man by the name of Khalid Abou El Fadl at UCLA School of Law concluded that women could lead mixed congregational prayers. "But I can't," I told Saleemah when we talked about it. "My Arabic isn't good enough."

"We must stop," she told me, "from discounting ourselves as unworthy or incapable. We have to embrace who we are and know that God is compassionate to our humanity." With her words, I realized that it was very true that we only did ourselves a disservice when we allowed our humanity to be a limitation for our ability to lead. I knew this very personally. My baby's conception out of wedlock had made me the target of attacks that I wasn't worthy of being a leader. A man wrote in an electronic discussion, "She should remain in the shadows." Should I? Was I unworthy of being a leader? I had never wanted to be a leader. I wanted to simply act true to my convictions and take *actions* for a better world, not just talk vacuously about it. It was dawning on me that, perhaps, that was in part what it meant to be a leader.

We won in Morgantown, and the event was covered widely in the national and international media. The leadership publicly affirmed the right of women to use the front door and main hall, and the first woman ever was elected to office at the mosque.

I was flirting with the notion that, for the first time in my life, I *wanted* to be a leader, when I received an email from Karamah, a Washington-based group of leading Muslim women lawyers organized to improve human rights. I had turned to it for help in the first days of my struggles with the mosque, but, to my disappointment, didn't hear back from the group. It was organizing a summer "leadership development program." I read its note carefully: "Despite the fact that women are being educated and trained in numbers equivalent to men, leadership and power tend to be male dominated especially when it comes to bringing about change in social, political and religious fields. This is particularly true for Muslim women in the U.S. and elsewhere. Many negative cultural messages have a strong impact on Muslim women, keeping them from playing an active role in their community's social development."

I remembered so many cultural cues that kept me from stepping forward as a leader: the silence of women in heady political discussions at dinners growing up, my cousins who got marriage licenses instead of the Ph.D.s they wanted, and the absence of women from the ranks of our community leaders. Then I received a double-edged email. It was the bold sermon of a Muslim leader in Chicago, Imam Abdul Malik Mujahid. He recognized the inequities women faced nationwide at mosques and called upon Muslim women to assemble a national task force. " 'Men's Islam' or Islam for all?" he asked. "While sisters are a full part of the community, many mosques are run as though Islam is just for men." He said: "It is time that sisters come together and provide leadership in clearly defining a Muslim women's manifesto for change in mosques in North America." Then, he added a caveat: "If these sisters are practicing Muslims, they will have a far higher level of success in demanding change and leading it." It was judgments about women as "practicing" or "not practicing" that so often made us feel unworthy. Who made these judgment calls? So often we let others make the decision about our self-worth, and I was starting to believe that it was ultimately our own personal responsibilities to defend our right to speak, to stand, and to fight for change. To his credit, he called for women to create a national women's caucus on the issues of women's rights in mosques. But, again, he added a caveat. They should be women "who are respected and honored by the community."

There was no room at the table, then, for the bad girls of Islam, as I and other women were being called. This cycle of making others illegitimate was one I knew well. I had become a volunteer at my local rape and domestic violence shelter and hot line service. In training one day, I examined the "Power and Control Wheel," a graphic model developed out of Duluth, Minnesota, chronicling the intimidation, social isolation, and emotional abuse women faced when they challenged husbands who abused them. I stared at the wheel, and I knew it applied to women who also challenged power and control in society. I was living the Power and Control Wheel in my life. It was only our own personal fortitude that could allow us to overcome all of the forces used to try to defeat us.

In my life, I was continuing to face assault from the men in power at my mosque. They put me on trial because thirty-five people had signed a petition to have me banned from the mosque for disturbing services. My sin: speaking up against the inequities. I knew, at this moment of true trial, that we will always face opposition when we want to lead social change. But it is the personal challenge of each one of us to persevere. For that reason, on trial at my hometown mosque, I stood before the national convention of the Islamic Society of North America and presented an Islamic Bill of Rights for Women in Mosques. It was simple but clear: We have a right to leadership, voice, and full self-expression at the mosque. We have a right to the front doors and the main halls of mosques. And we have a right to be protected from gossip and slander. Later, recognizing that our sexuality is often used against us, I wrote an Islamic Bill of Rights for Women in the Bedroom.

Sadly, that would be one of the deepest challenges we faced.

The Chicago imam released another sermon. This one was a eulogy to a pioneering Muslim woman leader, Sharifa Alkhateeb. I had met her as I was organizing the march to the mosque in Morgantown, and she had offered kind advice and guidance, always supportive and gracious. In the eulogy, the imam again tried to divide the women who were worthy of leadership from the ones he deemed not to be worthy. Singling me out, he noted that Sharifa had been "extremely disturbed" by me and my first book, a memoir in which I honestly discussed my struggles as a woman in Islam, facing judgment, narrow-mindedness, and sexist traditions. He acknowledged the inequities that drive Muslim women from their communities, but then, sadly, he tried again to drive a wedge into the American Muslim women's world. He celebrated Sharifa as a "great Muslim leader," and then he added, "The difference between today's 'me too Islamofeminist' and Shareefa," as he spelled her name, "is that Shareefa never strayed from the middle path of obedience to God while remaining defiant to men instead of becoming disobedient to God in her protest towards ignorant Muslim men. Of course she was Shareefa, the noble one."

The message was clear: the rest of us were the ignoble ones. I came out of the audience to stand up on the stage at the Gluck Theater on the campus of West Virginia University, speaking about my activism for women's rights at mosques. I introduced a Morgantown Model I had created, based on the Power and Control Wheel, of the harassment we can expect in any community when we become activists for social change. A Muslim woman raised her hand and, ignoring my 45-minute presentation, implemented the strategy always used to distract and destabilize us. Her question to me was: Didn't my baby make me unworthy of leadership? I listened to her patiently and told her what I had come to believe: "If I was married, I would be attacked for not covering my hair. If I covered my hair, I would be attacked for not speaking Arabic. If I spoke Arabic, I would be attacked for not speaking Arabic well enough. There will always be something to try to undermine us as leaders in our communities, but if not us, then who?"

I had learned that others' judgments define us only if we allow them to do so. In so many ways, I have felt under siege in the days since I ascended into the main hall of my mosque. Often, I wondered how I could survive. I came to appreciate a truth that a scholar of Islam, Amina Wadud, had told me. "In spiritual activism," she said, "you must separate the spiritual from the activism." Until we had fully transformed my mosque, I wasn't going to find peace there. I had to find it in my inner life. We must each build our own spiritual communities to sustain us through the trials of activism. To my shock, I received an invitation to join a retreat of Muslim leaders of tomorrow, organized by the ASMA Society's Daisy Khan and one of the women from the march to the mosque, Sarah Eltantawi. I was a leader? The girl who was always the secretary but never the president had become a leader without winning any election or title?

I found the answer most clearly in my son. In the months since I had first taken him to the mosque, he had learned to prostrate fully to surrender himself for a moment from the momentum of his life. He had learned to exhale "Allah hu"—a remembrance of God—with his spotting of the moon. He had learned to exclaim "Allahu Akbar," or "God is Great," even if he said it "Abababoo." I realized that we all have a safe part of our lives that we must nurture and protect when we dare to take risks and challenge conventions. It is our inner strength that allows us then to make the difficult choices that let us fully express the leader in all of us. I have to look no further than my son to remember this always. As we walked the other day, he exclaimed, "Mama! Hand!"

He slipped his soft hand into mine, as I curled my fingers over his, each one of us a leader for the other.

AN ISLAMIC BILL OF RIGHTS FOR WOMEN IN MOSQUES

Women have an Islamic right to enter a mosque.

Women have an Islamic right to enter through the main door.

Women have an Islamic right to visual and auditory access to the *musalla* (main sanctuary).

Women have an Islamic right to pray in the *musalla* without being separated by a barrier, including in the front and in mixed-gender congregational lines.

Women have an Islamic right to address any and all members of the congregation.

Women have an Islamic right to hold leadership positions, including positions as prayer leaders, or imams, and as members of the board of directors and management committees.

Women have an Islamic right to be full participants in all congregational activities.

Women have an Islamic right to lead and participate in meetings, study sessions, and other community activities without being separated by a barrier.

Women have an Islamic right to be greeted and addressed cordially.

Women have an Islamic right to respectful treatment and exemption from gossip and slander.

AN ISLAMIC BILL OF RIGHTS FOR WOMEN IN THE BEDROOM

Women have an Islamic right to respectful and pleasurable sexual experience.

Women have an Islamic right to make independent decisions about their bodies, including the right to refuse sexual advances.

Women have an Islamic right to make independent decisions about their partner, including the right to object to a husband marrying a second wife.

Women have an Islamic right to make independent decisions about their choice of a partner.

Women have an Islamic right to make independent decisions about contraception and reproduction.

Women have an Islamic right to protection from physical, emotional, and sexual abuse.

Women have an Islamic right to sexual privacy.

Women have an Islamic right to exemption from criminalization or punishment for consensual adult sex.

Women have an Islamic right to exemption from gossip and slander.

Women have an Islamic right to sexual health care and sex education.

PART IV **SOUL JOURNEYS**

One of the surprising outcomes of editing this anthology was the discovery that for many of the contributors, myself included, alienation from the mainstream Muslim community was a prerequisite to our personal spiritual transformation. In order to develop our relationship with God, we needed to leave the community for a period of time. Our leaving was largely the result of being judged and marginalized within our existing religious community. Many of the submissions in this section offer a look into our spiritual evolution.

And on these soul journeys each contributor searches for the face of the divine feminine in Islam. While the divine feminine exists in the Jewish and Christian legs of the Abrahamic stool and in many traditions throughout the world, we Muslims have forgotten her face in the Islamic tradition. American Muslim women must reclaim our abundant tradition of female spiritual masters. Central to the evolution of Muslim culture, indeed of world culture in general, is the reclamation of feminine divine energy to address the toxicity resulting from its suppression. Muslims and the world need to see the face of the feminine divine.

Mary, mother of Jesus, Rabia of Basra, and Fatima, daughter of Prophet Muhammad, were a few women of unshakable faith who left a legacy of spiritual mastery for women and men. To represent American Muslim women reclaiming our historical female leaders, the cover of this anthology has a hand of Fatima, a symbol used to ward off the evil eye but also a beautiful reminder of the powerful legacy of the feminine face in Islam.

In this section an activist trained in philosophy meditates on Islam, a young performer claims her gift of song, and an autistic boy teaches his mother about God. We also have a poem about an African female saint from the Shi'a tradition and a closing prayer for all Muslim women composed by a woman who was born Palestinian, born black.

A MEDITATION ON THE CLEARING

Sarah Eltantawi

In thinking about Islam, I tend to focus so much on my struggles within it (around gender, chauvinism, and intolerance) that I often fail to feel the presence of the more essential question beneath my struggle to uncover Islam: Why, in the first place, do I find myself engaging in this effort? In my struggle to understand why it is that I care so deeply about Islam, I find myself needing to engage in clearing the weeds that block my sight, preventing me from traveling down an Islamic path, one of many paths, toward the truth about the nature of creation and the subsequent lives we should lead as a result. I often find myself drawing an analogy between Islam and love: both nontactile, both educing overwhelming emotion, but both fragile and susceptible to being ruined by the slightest indelicacy. The Palestinian poet Mahmoud Darwish writes that his daily cup of coffee at dawn becomes instantly rancid at the sound of a voice. Imagine the potential to sully Islam.

I am calling Islam—and this short, strange life, this blessed and absurd earth, our beings trapped as we are by our bodies and the limits of our mind—a forest. Ego-inspired tendencies toward judgment and arrogance, I call weeds.

There is a simple, historical answer to why I care about Islam: 9/11, an instance in time where my being was seized by a historical moment in which I had no choice but to respond by seizing that moment back. For all intents and purposes a query-filled agnostic circa September 10, 2001, I found myself one of a handful of people defending Islam and Muslims on national television before a terrified, angry, and confused audience starting on September 11. Trained in the Western liberal tradition and brought up an unreflective Muslim, I suppose that positioning made sense. Today, I have only begun to understand that the thrust into this particular forest, or world, was not mere coincidence, not simply a professional imperative.

So there is a forest, a world, a path, a magnetic pull, and it is called Islam, and I am in it surrounded by weeds. At that point in time when I actually clear the Islamic forest for myself of the weeds like sexism, chauvinism, and judgment, what will be left? Where and what is Islamic purity? Where and what is the truth? And how does it relate to my searching soul?

The Clearing

In seeking the truth, we very rarely come upon a clearing. In college, my friends and I would take hikes along the beautiful northern California coastline and let out excited shouts cloaked in protective sarcasm when we came upon a clearing in the forest: "The truth!" We attempted to locate meaning in the relative calm and emptiness of that clearing in the forest, an unconstrained space where trees did not choose to sprout, offering a natural meeting point for us to converge.

In the hustle and intensity that has colored life since 9/11, having relocated from northern California to Boston to Washington, D.C., and now New York City, I find that the clearing opens itself to me in fits and starts, almost always arriving in the form of an emotional interruption to what is invariably a busy day of catching subways, being on conference calls, preparing for talks, traveling, or taking time out to laugh with friends or family. Being as undisciplined and uncertain as I am about prayer, I sense that perhaps when I succeed in cutting more weeds, I may be able to create this clearing as many as five times a day, but I certainly can't force it. And yet, the clearing manifests. Rarely, for example, does the call to prayer, recited over a loudspeaker, or quietly to a congregation, fail to move me, sending me instantly inside myself to a place of contemplation.

Truth, the eternal, divine directive, is the clearing. How long have I longed to experience love for the Creator? My relationship with the Creator, perhaps like the relationship one has with one's self, is so close as to be piercingly sensitive; at times combative, at times calm, always relevant—but for me, by no means settled. I suppose the only abiding proof I have that I want to love the Creator in the first place is the unquenchable will I possess to find the clearing.

As if on cue, enter the self-doubts—internal, smaller weeds that wind around my heart, shielding one vessel from another, preventing continuity, eluding "Om," hiding the Creator, masking the forest. Maybe I'm just a disaffected, urban, single twenty-something who, while very busy, has too much mental space to mull over, complicate, and render abstract something that many suggest is utterly simple. The simple answer eludes me. So many of my friends have rigorously pursued the path of intoxicated agnosticism, within which I appreciate a certain honesty. And yet this path is unsettling, unless one is disciplined about one's agnosticism, passionate about the conviction that one can not know, seeking to study at least the attempts at knowing while maintaining critical distance. I must add that, paradoxically, it is worth the struggle to locate peace.

The Weeds

It is useful to meditate upon the roots of the weeds that have blocked my Islam. Here I will describe some personal experiences from childhood that gave me a problematic understanding of Islam, one that emphasized punishment, ritual for ritual's sake, and superstition misunderstood as religion. This is by no means to suggest that my experience with my immediate family vis-à-vis Islam was a negative one—quite the contrary. Some of my sweetest memories are of Ramadan in my house, where my brother and

I would return from school, my parents from work, and we would cook, often relatively quietly, due to lack of food and water, awaiting the magic hour where color would be restored to a world turned black-and-white, contemplative. Often in the minutes leading up to *iftar* (the breaking of the fast), we would stop talking altogether and put on a tape of Qur'anic recitation, allowing the beauty of the words to mingle with the scent of food preparation. And then there would be the unadulterated joy of eating, talking, and reflecting on the effects of fasting, which was explained to us by my parents as an exercise primarily in understanding how the poor felt. In recent years, in the intermittent times that I've fasted, I've tried to locate the spiritual side of fasting, and hope to be more successful in the future. Perhaps I will find more success as I succeed in clearing more weeds, a subject to which I will now turn.

To begin with, somewhere along the line, quite early on, I developed a major fear of the Qur'an. One of my earliest memories is of myself in conversation with the Qur'an at about the age of five or six. I was lying in bed in my room decorated with a '70s orange floral print, with the white bedside lamp turned on and the Qur'an on my lap. Fear paralyzed me. I used to play a game where I opened the Qur'an to a random page and read the verse, closed the book, opened it again and read another random verse. By design, my conspiratorial mind surmised, most of the verses I turned to seemed to be discussing the finer points of hell. On top of this, hell seemed to be a major topic of conversation in my family, a place where I was sure to go if I disobeyed my parents by playing too much dodge ball on the street with the neighborhood kids, wore shorts that were too short, or fought with my brother. After a while, the promise of hell for any and all minor offenses rendered the threat of it all but meaningless to my brother and me, who began to laugh when my mother would describe God burning off our skin and supplying new skin so that we could burn in hell forever. After a while, even my mom would laugh as she iterated hyperbolic, fantastic modes of punishment that were so obviously folkloric relics from the Egyptian culture she came from. She eventually stopped evoking these hellish images; perhaps for her, too, they began to fade in relevance, or maybe necessity, as her kids grew up. My mother's forays into rhetorical hell had a kind of adorable quality to them as I grew older, but as a child who tended to take things literally, they often made the world a scary and absurd place.

But Islam itself was always treated with reverence and respect in my family, especially by my father. Not quiet, subtle, or reserved in general, my father was rather private about his religious practices, retreating into the prayer room without forcing, or even asking, us to join him. As a child, I remember riding on his back as he knelt down, and I would flip over and practice the moves I learned in my tumbling class. My dad never stopped me from using his praying back as a springboard for my amateur gymnastics. In fact, my father never forced Islam in any way on my brother and me, despite the fact that he was a pious and otherwise fairly opinionated man. He had a way of characterizing life as harsh, reflecting, I think, his struggles as an immigrant and a man in this society, but for him Islam seemed to offer a place of beauty and rest. For my part, I knew intuitively that the beautifully bound book with gold lettering in this fascinating-looking script was somehow as much a part of my composition as the mysterious blood vessels and bones inside me that I could barely comprehend.

Noticing my fascination with the squiggly, incomprehensible script, my father presented me with the most impossibly thick book I had ever seen: Yusef Ali's English translation of the Qur'an. The smell of the paper, a sweet must, is embedded forever in my consciousness, as are the somehow already yellowing pages with Arabic on the right side, English on the left. At the bottom were a slew of footnotes that were almost always as thick as the verses and their translations above. I asked my father what the footnotes were. "What this man says the Qur'an means. Never mind it," he replied. Here I believe my father was communicating his conviction that the interpretations of man (perhaps meaning "man" literally, for my benefit as a daughter) were secondary to my own understanding of the text.

But what is a book in a strange script, one that opened the "wrong" way, when we disconnect it from the activities and practices of Muslims? I would argue, simply words on a page. Therefore, at a young age, a major influence of "lived" Islam for me was my maternal grandmother, Bahia Ma'awad Amin Mahgoub Salam (she kept four last names from her personal family lineage but, in accordance with Islamic tradition, never took on my grandfather's).

My grandmother, whom we call Mama Sito, would come spend months with us in California, and I would find morbid delight in listening to her dramatic stories of what God did to children who did not listen to their parents—how you could wake up and find your parents gone . . . how you should avoid shocking your parents with your bad behavior, because a woman who lived next door to her in her childhood village dropped dead of a heart attack the moment she learned that her daughter was marrying a man she did not approve of. As my grandmother, a strong-willed, ambitious, witty, and formidable woman, grew older, I watched her boisterously grapple with the reality of death. While my brother and I were at school, my grandmother would sit outside with our poodle as protection and company, speaking to him all day in Arabic, swatting him with her cane if he came too close to her while she was praying, and feeding him boiled eggs and fava beans. Mama Sito absolutely hated the quiet streets of the Los Angeles suburb we lived in, and she would complain that she wanted to return to Egypt, where the "dirt was sweet and the people were alive."

She was (and still is, though she's since suffered a stroke) one of the most quick-witted, brave, self-directed, and intelligent people I knew. At the age of seven, she forced herself into school when her mother was disinclined to educate her, stealing money from her purse and buying herself a slate, chalk, white socks with frills, and two pink ribbons for her hair. She then presented herself at the principal's office, where she demanded to be put in a classroom, offering up the change from her purchases as a down payment. The stunned principal promptly enrolled her, and after several months told my great-grandmother. She would tell me stories of how at a young age she would jump into the dense waters of the Nile, her hair, braided in two thick braids, floating on the surface as she swam. As she told me these stories, she would grow quiet, in mourning that her aging body would never again allow such a swim to be possible.

My grandmother negotiated these tragedies of life and death by placing her faith entirely in God, by believing deeply and unwaveringly that there was a master plan. Interestingly, this fatalism did not necessarily translate into comfort or acceptance of life's tragedies—she would always suffer every blow as a fresh wound, even as she approached eighty. Of further interest to me was the fact that she never seemed to translate this sensitivity to life's tragedies into anger at God. To God she only turned for help. I think this fatalism, coupled with sensitivity and emotion, made Mama Sito very strong; someone truly attentive to life as it is lived while simultaneously anchoring herself in an awareness of life's essentially fleeting nature.

As the years progressed, Mama Sito began talking to herself more. I walked into the living room one day and found her sitting as she so regally did on "her" chair—which was always perfumed and stocked (in the crevices of the cushions) with Kleenex, lotion, prayer beads, the newspaper, a Qur'an—talking to herself. Every day like clockwork, after Asr (midafternoon) prayer, Mama Sito would sit down in her chair, drink a cup of strong, sweet tea, and have a cigarette. She had assumed this familiar position one day when I heard, *"Akh! Akh! Ya Rab! Ya Rabie! Shamsie ba'yinzil. Shamsie ba'yinzil"* "Oh! Oh! Oh God! Oh God! My sun is setting. My sun is setting." I walked over and put my head on her lap, burying my head in her abundant chest, and said in my childish Arabic, "Don't worry, Mama Sito, why would God hate you? Why would he put you in hell? You? You raised five kids, you tried your best, you always remembered God, you've never hurt anyone." Mama Sito cried and cried and cried, and the tears turned into sobs. "Come with me in the kitchen," she said. When we arrived, she took out of the oven a pan of okra and potatoes she had made for us, then called for my brother, who had considerably less patience with Mama Sito's angst, preferring instead to crack endless jokes that would make even her laugh. "Put your hand in the oven!" she instructed us, and we did, with my brother laughing hysterically the entire time. It was hot, and we told her so in no uncertain terms. "If you think this is hot, imagine hell!!" she replied, whereupon she again broke into uncontrollable sobs.

One day, as I lay in bed playing the "read a random verse" game, I came upon a verse that would change my life forever:

> Men are in charge of women, because Allah hath made the one of them to excel the other, and because they spend of their property [for the support of women]. So good women are the obedient, guarding in secret that which Allah hath guarded. As for those from whom ye fear rebellion, admonish them and banish them to beds apart, and scourge them. Then if they obey you, seek not a way against them. Lo! Allah is ever High, Exalted, Great. [4:34]

I marched into my parents' bedroom and demanded to know the meaning of this. I could tell two things: one, my father hadn't thought about it much, and didn't have the heart or will to try and corroborate the verse, and two, my mom didn't believe a word of it. Their response to my insistent demands ended up being, "Just keep reading and learning more." Great. Men are stronger than women? How so? I wondered. The only thing I could come up with was muscles, which was the only explanation my mom offered. That night I fell asleep, picturing a man in the sky sitting on a throne, staring sternly down on me, waiting for me to mess up, to think the wrong thought or do the wrong thing. In an obvious reference to the patriarchy embedded in the life of a young girl from the earliest age, if not at conception, I literally thought God was my grandfather, a chain-smoking poet/

essayist of few words who was part of a Sufi order in Cairo and whom I met only briefly in Egypt before he died. The man in the sky—Baba Gido, as we called my grandfather—was watching over my every move, listening to each secret thought, all the while severely judging me and writing my deeds down in a giant book: a plus sign for everything I did right, a minus for everything I did wrong.

Very stressful stuff for a kid. I think that very early on, I stopped believing that this crude tallying of positives and negatives could really be the way it was, and I knew that my grandmother's suffering was unfair and neurotic. It wasn't until college, however, that I began to shake off many of the major pieces of folklore, patriarchy, and authoritarianism that I had been taught at the local mosque, and to some extent at home, was Islam. As to be expected at a place like Berkeley, where I was an undergraduate student, these forays into self-discovery and paganism could reach considerable extremes. Almost all of my friends were in one way or another "recovering" Catholics, Hindus, Confucianists, Jews, or Muslims. We banded together largely on this basis, making extensive fun of all things orthodox, and doggedly pursued alternatives to the "opiate of the masses" (Marx), the "tyranny of the weak against the strong" (Nietzsche), the mullahs, those who manipulated truth in pursuit of power (Foucault), patriarchy and heterosexism, and those we uncharitably called the "Jesus freaks," or guitar-playing, proselytizing Christians on campus who were the target of much derision and ridicule. It was at Berkeley that I discovered the secular world—salvation through art, music, philosophy, poetry, good food, and other pleasures.

Utopia, alas, was fleeting, and so, about six years after graduation, I was on the phone with a good friend one morning at 3:00 A.M. when I revisited the question of the Qur'an. Of course, by that point I had been working in the Muslim community for three years, but in the post-9/11 era, work in the Muslim community for me revolved around politics, the protection of civil liberties, immigration issues, wrestling with guys like Bill O'Reilly and Daniel Pipes, and other nonsacred priorities. But the spiritual questions that had captivated me since childhood never went away—they found expression in college in secular terms, but were now tugging at me again in the midst of New York urban life.

I shouldn't have been on the phone that night, since I had to go to Washington, D.C., in a matter of hours to attend a meeting with House Democratic leader Nancy Pelosi that evening, and I was up late getting work done for the meeting. As is often the case when I have an incredible amount of work to do within a short span of time, I found myself in a long, intense conversation about a topic unrelated to the activity at hand—this time, the Qur'an. My friend, an agnostic who considers himself a cultural Muslim, often says he doesn't believe "a word" of any of the texts. He asked me a fundamental question that left me stuck—what was my position on scripture? At that moment, the Qur'an that I always keep on my nightstand, resting on an engraved wooden book holder, caught my eye. Whether I liked it or not, whether I read it or not, the Qur'an was the most important book in my life. Why? My friend and I began to discuss this. For him, study of the Qur'an had always been an endeavor for the learned, an undertaking pursued only by the erudite, though not necessarily an *alim* or explicitly religious scholar. For me, the Qur'an was always presented as something folksy, a grassroots guideline for each and every person, a text that was distinguished in precisely this way from great works of literature or philosophy. Essentially, Qur'anic studies were perceived by the two of us as the exclusive domain of the elite and as the ultimate text of the everyday person. It was fascinating to me that one text could be imagined so differently in different communities over time and space. I realized that the sheer impact that this book had—spiritually, sociologically, and politically—as an objective matter made it easily the most important book in my life.

I began to meditate on this further. At some level, any text that professes to give guidance to life's vexing questions becomes a reference point from which one asks oneself major questions. The Qur'an, for Muslims, is the ultimate reference point. For American Muslims, these times are exciting ones in which the boundaries of what it means to be a Muslim—in terms of identity, specific forms of practice or nonpractice, sectarian affiliation or nonaffiliation, and attitudes about major social issues, including gender roles—is expanding before our eyes. We live in a time where an unbeliever of Muslim heritage feels the need to call herself or himself a Muslim, in the way Sartre said, "In the face of anti-Semitism, I am a Jew."

Yet something that I find fascinating in my observations is that even those on the furthest point of the margins away from orthodoxy, nonetheless reference themselves in one way or another to Islam, even if that means positioning oneself as a total unbeliever, the radical opposite of what is traditionally thought of as a Muslim. This inherent limitedness of reference points has a presence in Western philosophy as well. Could it be that as human beings, we are as limited by basic concepts as we are by our bodies? In this sense of what seems to be the inherent limitedness of ideas, therefore, the Qur'an is the most important book in the world for an expanded definition of Muslims. It cannot, and will not, be dismissed, even by the most hardened of us.

A Clearing

Muslims, like all people, like flowers, are diverse; no two Muslims are alike. Muslims also respond in different ways to the institutions that call themselves Islamic, including mosques. One Friday, a friend who was visiting me in New York from Los Angeles wanted to attend *juma* prayers. On the few occasions when I am driven toward *juma* prayers, I attend a Sufi mosque. But that Friday afternoon, as New York was graced with late summer breezes, my usual mosque was closed, and so at the late hour of 1:00 P.M. my friend and I jumped in a cab and sped across town to make the *khutba* at another location.

As I was ushered up to the balcony of the mosque, where the women were isolated from the men, my view of the imam was blocked by a lime green wall of geometric shapes. I felt the familiar exclusion and disgust at such unjustifiable sexism. I felt that my dignity had been compromised, once again, for the thousandth time, in stark contradiction to the Qur'an, which asserts:

> We have conferred dignity on the children of Adam, and borne them over land and sea, and provided for them sustenance out of the good things of life, and favored them far above most of our Creations. [17:70]

I searched for the strength of my mother, my grandmother, but just felt fed up and pissed off. I felt the gnarled, menacing weeds sprout before me, this time lime green in color, just as unwelcome. I thought back to the protest of a mosque I had participated in months before in Morgantown, West Virginia, where I and five other Muslim women walked in through the male-only front entrance, in the presence of quite a few journalists. I remembered how mixed my feelings were during that event, how I cried when I saw the men in the mosque looking anxiously out the window, scared of the media attention, worried about their mosque, perhaps about their families. I felt horrible that I had participated in bringing this trouble to the mosque, but knew that it had to be done. Now I was reacquainted with the rage that prompted me to protest—the strident objection of my soul to being shoved in a corner in what purported to be the house of Allah. Like an idol, such foolish, cowardly injustice had to be smashed, for our own good, male and female. Yanking off my hijab in unconscious defiance after prayer, I looked around for my male companion, seeing red, filled with revolutionary vehemence. It was time to get in a cab, get out of there and go to the park, where I was not going to be shoved up a tree. Where was my friend? I was starting to feel slightly uncomfortable without a male companion, feeling eyes on me as I wandered around.

There he was, happily taking pictures of the minaret, shaking hands with a brother, looking completely at ease. I could not help but smile. He, like the vast majority of all other men, had no idea how I felt. I couldn't be mad at him, I could only marvel at the difference in his experience, even laughing inside at how stark the contrast was. Catching my eye, he cheerfully said, "Here, Sarah, stand in front of the minaret, I want to practice taking a picture with 'the building and a person.' " He had a new digital camera he was obsessed with that had pre-settings for pictures. I obliged, and as he finished taking the picture, we saw the cutest little girl. She was a toddler, with huge, chubby cheeks, wearing a coordinated, red-and-white plaid outfit with the cutest hat. That girl had been my only source of comfort when I was in a state of near-total agitation earlier during the prayer. We asked her mother's permission and started to take pictures of her walking around, grabbing my water bottle, looking confused and smiling. I was starting to relax. I was even starting to enjoy myself. I found myself saying *in sha' allah* and *salam alaikum* and calling people "sister" and "brother," actions I am not inclined to take when I am in a state of fury over gender issues, when I am choked by a weed. I longed not to have to contrast the freedom of mingling in the open courtyard with Muslims with the stifling environment of the balcony.

Other people, men and women, walked by and smiled at the little girl, and smiled at us. We were still in the courtyard of the mosque, which I started to notice was very beautiful. I was not wearing hijab, and I felt totally comfortable. I suddenly realized that in the outer sphere of the mosque, when the prayers were over and lines disbanded and I could climb down those damn steps, I had entered a clearing. Before I knew it, I was in a space where good feelings were allowed to flow, where I was not being shoved away, implicitly accused of preying sexually on the spiritual concentration of men, where I could enjoy the company of fellow Muslims who had taken time out of their workday to remember the Creator, which was, after all, a beautiful thing to do. I have such nice memories of that courtyard, the slight breeze, the little girl, the beautiful engraving on the outside of the mosque, the tree I stood by to take the picture, the smiling faces— black, brown, white, yellow—as they walked out of the mosque's courtyard.

As we left, my friend commented *"Takabul Allah"* (May God accept your prayer). *Takabul Allah.* This was a beautiful thing to utter after prayer, to be sure. Would we see a day where I could freely say this to anyone around me after prayer?

Recently in Brooklyn, a friend of mine was excitedly showing me the garden in her new apartment. Expecting to find tomato groves, red peppers, basil, and rosemary, I was shocked to find the most overgrown mess of foliage I had ever seen, a truly alarming sight. "It needs work," she offered. "Yeah," I concurred. I could not see past the beginning of the garden to the outer perimeter, couldn't tell what was on the other side. I found myself somewhat frightened, and certainly intimidated—I was afraid of what I could not see, afraid of that which blocked my sight. After years of blockage, I could imagine myself resenting what's on the other side, and convincing myself that it doesn't matter anyway. Do those who construct these boundaries know the damage they do?

Clearing the Weeds for Good

There is a Sufi saying to the effect that, as we human beings walk, we find boulders in our path, which we pick up and toss behind us into a bag that we carry on our back. Eventually the bag becomes too heavy, and we can no longer walk. It then becomes time to dump the bag. I want to dump the bag. But how, when there continue to be boulders? The only solution, it seems, is to take another path, one with fewer rocks, fewer weeds. If that means ceasing to attend those mosques that practice gender apartheid, so be it. I can no longer suffer it out of defiance. I am looking for a clearing that conflates Islam with the truth and the truth with life as it is lived. Life as it is lived is reality, and reality, so far as it comes from God, is holy.

My struggle is to cease experiencing God as the "village tyrant" in an Arab or South Asian village, as a friend of mine so astutely put it (and I never even told him stories of my grandmother).

Islam is an integral part of my experience as this particular subjective self. If God has breathed his essence into each of us, it follows that we should search within ourselves for answers, for insight. It further follows that the answer to the question about whether it's "OK" or "relevant" to listen to one's soul, is yes, for within us rests a breath of God. May God be generous in God's help and mercy—the path is not an easy one, full of rocks and weeds, and the clearings, at least for now, are few and far between. But when the clearings emerge, they offer enough cool water, laughter, and beauty to keep going, and going, onward toward our final meeting with the truth.

A SIREN SONG

Aroosha Zoq Rana

The stage lights spark warmth and energy into the dark space. A tingle begins in my toes, sweeps through the base of my feet, and grounds me in a comfortable stance. Rooted energy spirals through my lower body, gaining momentum from the excited butterflies in my stomach. Surging through the lungs, vibrating off the vocal cords, soaring up the throat, articulating past the tongue and lips comes my sound—my truth in the form of breath, tone, and rhythm. I step forward, take hold of the microphone, glance back at my ensemble, and journey through the performance sharing my creative energy with all present in the room. I feel good. I feel alive. I feel complete.

This description, full of passion and vitality, is not how I've always felt about performance. In the past, I believed that my desire to share my creativity with others was at odds with my identity as a Muslim woman. Since my youth I was taught to believe that women and performance do not mix, because a female performer excites lust, desire, and impure thoughts.

There is a belief among Muslims that a woman is *"awrah."* In Arabic, *awrah,* meaning "damaging," has a pejorative connotation. This strain of Islamic ideology submits that because a woman is *awrah,* her presence, her voice, her existence is negative and brings harm. The result is that she must be covered and hidden, and her voice should not be heard, lest it corrupt those who listen.

I remember being seven years old and having my father videotape me singing songs that I learned in chorus to send to my relatives in Pakistan. I reenacted routines from school and choreographed my own movements to made-up melodies. I recall my parents laughing in the background as I performed these little song-and-dance numbers. At times my mom broke in with her crackly alto tones and my dad made up Urdu parodies to English songs in his velvety baritone voice. Fun and carefree, the rehearsals and recitals brought us together. One day during one of our escapades, my grandmother stopped me mid-song and forbid me from engaging in such behavior again. Shocked, I couldn't understand what I had done wrong. I thought I had found fans in my father's friend and his sons, who played the part of my first audience. Our eyes met and I saw a flicker of my own disbelief reflected in the youngest son's eyes before he turned to look at his father. My father broke the awkward silence with a joke as I slipped out of the living room. Later that evening, my mother sat me down and told me a story that my grandmother told her when she had been close to my age.

It was the story of Noor...

The finest silks adorned her well-kept figure. Choosing a deep blue tone to complement the silver gray of the evening, she carefully selected her outfit for the evening's festivities. And adding the final touches of her kohl eyeliner, she adjusted the gauzy-thin scarf on her head and floated down the steps leading from her inner chambers to the outer courtyard of her home. Tonight she would be entertaining one of India's largest landowners in the Punjabi province. Like her sisters before her, and her mother before them, Noor earned her living by entertaining courtly patrons. In sweet tones and dramatic melodies she crooned her sorrows and delights and took her visitor to another level of consciousness. Entranced by her music and yearning for more, the privileged guest asked to be escorted to her inner chambers for a more intimate sort of song and dance.

My mother finished her story saying that my grandmother only wanted the best for me, and she wanted people to see me as a decent girl. My grandmother feared that my performance in front of men who were not part of my household would mar my reputation within the South Asian community. In short, my love of song and dance relegated me to the realm of a prostitute. This marked my experience feeling bad about wanting to sing. Of course, I did not want to hurt my grandmother or behave indecently, so I began performing for female-only audiences.

But that did not last for long. As the blessed Prophet Muhammad taught, *to know yourself is to know your Lord,* therefore as a Muslim it is my duty to honor the spirit within me. I carry Islam in the depths and folds of my inner being. To truly understand myself and tap my human potential, I need to discover my inner divinity, and honor it. Ever since I can remember, singing and being on stage has moved me to a place where I feel a natural high. When I open my mouth to sing, I am able to communicate my love for this world to those around me.

Then how could I, by the sheer fact that I perform, be connected to the actions of Noor from my grandmother's story, and how could this mere connection make me a bad Muslim girl? Since my days of Islamic Sunday school I learned that before praying, fasting, or embarking on any journey, you must develop an intention. The intention equaled the action in importance, and as long as I set my intentions with Allah's mercy and benevolence in mind, I could trust my actions. When singing, I never intended to exploit myself or corrupt others. On the contrary, motivation to perform came from within me, not from external influences.

I had to devise a way to continue doing what I loved, so before hitting puberty, I learned how to cultivate one aspect of my femininity—negotiating space. Khadija, the first woman to convert to Islam, is a powerful example of a woman who thrived as a successful businesswoman despite the male-dominated reality of her society. A wealthy woman, she proposed marriage to the Prophet Muhammad, a man fifteen years her junior. I called on the powerful example of her life to empower me. Khadija used her natural feminine ability to negotiate space for herself within the society and to thrive in her business. I admired this trait and often found myself experimenting with social skills that allowed my natural negotiation skills to flourish. In time I used this power by surrounding myself with a comfortable and supportive circle of people. I shied away from performing around Muslims who might judge me harshly, and by the time I began performing in musicals, choirs, and solo concerts in high school, I knew who to include in my support circle.

To be honest, I did not feel totally comfortable doing this. Being confident about my identity as a performer but not being able to acknowledge that openly seemed like a contradiction of intentions. I could share my art and be true to myself, but only on a limited scale. I had yet to figure out how to negotiate and create safe spaces without compromising a part of myself in the process. I knew myself, but fought that knowledge. Leading a double existence, I ran around in figure eight patterns just waiting for the instances where the two loops would touch together. Strong in my faith, I decided to cover my hair and wear hijab. Ready to share my love and respect for Islam with the world, I hoped this physical act would allow me to openly display what lay in my heart. Although concerned about what people might say about a hijab-wearing performer, I expected that it would prove my loyalty and commitment to those around me, and that would make me feel better about the crisscrossed notion of my identity.

One evening during a performance with my high school a cappella group, bobbing alongside my peers, I threw myself into a rendition of an 80s pop tune. We had spent hours rehearsing the piece, but we sang it as if it were the first time. I looked around the U-shaped formation and laughed at the duo at the end doing a Madonna-like dance move. As a corner of my headscarf fell forward, I quickly threw it across my shoulder, and in that split second I realized that I had donned hijab for all the wrong reasons. I looked out into the crowd trying to find my mother; she sat there with a smile. Earlier that day she had questioned my reason for wearing hijab and asked if the experience fulfilled my intention. I smiled at her now, thinking how even though I had not responded, she had given me a hug and told me that she would always support me in my decisions, but that true support comes from within.

I had hoped that wearing hijab and openly declaring my faith in Islam would make my life decisions easier, but at that moment I realized I put it on as an outward reflection of my inner being—as a symbol to prove my faith to others. But really, I was hoping that it would prove something to myself; that it would clarify my identity as a Muslim woman, strengthen my relationship to the Creator, and stop me from doing anything that did not fall in alignment with Islam—such as performing. I felt closer to God than ever before in my life. Wearing the folds of fabric made me stronger in my resolve to be true to what lay within the folds of my heart and soul. With this confusion, I decided to stop wearing hijab—to not use it as a shield to hide behind to suppress my desire to be on stage and stifle my creativity.

The drive within me to honor my creativity juxtaposed against the external pull of my fear of judgment became unbearable. I yearned to embrace myself and have all components of my character—woman, artist, Muslim—meld into one unified identity. As I headed off to college, hundreds of miles away from my family and my circle of comfort, I suddenly found myself alone, in a new setting, with new boundaries to negotiate. To be true to my inner self I learned that I had to take care of myself first and foremost. I took classes that stimulated my mind and joined campus groups that made me feel active within the community. I auditioned for an a cappella group and started performing within my first month on campus. I made time for arts and crafts and went to see concerts and museum exhibits on a regular basis. Cultivating my artist self made me feel alive and fresh, and it strengthened my relationship with Islam because I devoted time and energy to knowing myself first. And the best feeling of all was that I was just being me.

During my third year in college, an interesting interaction with a Muslim peer of mine showed me how much I had grown. She chose to audition for a slot in my a cappella group. Seeing her in the audience of almost every concert for the previous three years, I knew she had wanted to join for a very long time. She had a great energy, and everyone in the group immediately responded to her infectious laughter. Her sound reflected the joy she felt when singing. Seeing my old self in her shoes and excited to share this experience with her, I let her know how happy I was to sing with her. Toward the end of her second audition, she pulled me aside and asked me how I faced the Muslim community while performing with the group. She explained that her brother and his friends had discouraged her from auditioning because performance by a female is forbidden in Islam. I asked her to describe to me what her intentions were when she sang. She told me that she wanted to create something fun, feel good about it, and share that with her friends and family. I asked if any of that broke any rules in Islam. She replied, "No, of course not," and then I replied, "Well, there's your answer."

Islam embodies a beautiful faith which holds each person accountable for his or her intentions and actions, and only Allah has the ultimate role in judgment. It took me a long time to figure this out, and once I started being true to my inner being I found that most of my fear and hesitation disappeared. I found a way to negotiate my Muslim experience and express myself as an artist because I know myself and treat myself as I would treat anything divine. Physically—I cannot hide behind hijab or acceptance from my community. I must be comfortable in my own skin and embrace my existence. Mentally—I challenge myself not to fear. I am clear about my intentions when I perform and trust myself. I treat my thoughts as being divine and honor them. I understand that I am only human and must be able to assess, forgive, accept, learn, and move on. Spiritually—I reflect on the basis of my actions and intentions. I evaluate the level of control let go in order to flow with the rhythm of my creativity and the breath of my Creator. I feel at peace with myself. I have found my personal pathway to the divine within, and this allows me to cultivate my identity as a Muslim woman with a full sense of confidence and contentment. Any sense of fear or hesitation floats away and I feel heavenly—moved to sing praises of the *paradise that lies at the feet of the mother.*

When I think of paradise I think of a space where nature's sounds, scents, and caresses weave in and out of ethereal existence. I imagine a place where cool rains, warm sunshine, and dancing moonbeams play together. A place where honey-water soothes the heat of the sands and the tumbling waves sound like babbling babies. In this paradise resides the divine feminine spirit, standing firm and easy on the smooth, red rock in the purple fray. Crooning to the ebb and flow of the swirling celestial pool, her siren song beckons compatriots in the faithful struggle to spread goodness and spark flames of positive action. Her siren song wails an affirmation of trust and inspiration to support me, nurture my wounds, fill my heart with love, and send me on my journey—satisfied, full, and yet hungry for more.

BLESSED DIVINE WOMAN

Sham-e-Ali al-Jamil

Hadrat Fatima Masumah,
your holy shrine
resides in the middle
of this city
like a heart
sustaining life,
sanctuary on saline earth,
clear blue solace.

Tonight,
rose water moistens
arid air,
strings of lights
shine like small
flowers glowing,
it is the anniversary
of your arrival to *Qum,*
You, whose presence
made this city
a holy place.

'Aalimah,
Learned Scholar,
I press my forehead gently
against the entrance
to your sanctuary,
smooth wooden door
cools my mind
as I humbly request
your permission
to enter.

In the sanctity
of this space,
pilgrims' supplications reflect
again and again against
intricate mirror work above,
prayers, gratitude and
tears blend
like scarlet blue
smears of color at dusk,
where our spirits
take rest
for a moment.

Of the million people
who visit your holy grave,
where wishes and hopes
grow like seedling trees,
where we weep
as we request
your intercession,
Gracious Healer,
we feel heard.

With my heart released
in this refuge,
next to other women
their children
grandmothers with *tasbeh,*
the smell of sweat and roses
whispers of prayer
I close my eyes, thankful
hold this memory
of *ziyarat,* close
a salve,
for wounded days.

MY SON THE MYSTIC

Inas Younis

Sometimes it takes a matter of the heart to cure the rigidity of a rule-centered mind. For many women, myself included, the meaning of life did not originate in the heart or mind but from the maternal womb, where I experienced my first and most profound realization—a realization best expressed by a woman who once accurately remarked that to decide to have children is to resolve to have your heart forever go walking around outside your body. The reality of that assertion was one I have never quarreled with, believing that, as a Muslim woman, I was obliged to inevitably relinquish my entire heart in reverence to the divine ideals of love and sacrifice. It was also a reality that compelled me to adopt the attitude that brains are not only inconvenient, but detrimental in a woman.

This viewpoint, which was a basic feature of my strict religious outlook, presented only two scenarios worth exploring in the enterprise of my life: either to gratify my heart's highest calling through motherhood, or to bear the responsibilities of a liberated mind. And when observance of my credo compelled me to establish a preference between my overactive mind or my duty-bound heart, I of course chose the latter.

Ironically, it was not until I emigrated with my family from Iraq to the United States that I assumed a more visible Islamic identity—an identity that served as an antidote to the modern secularism which was the unwritten state-enforced "religion" of my homeland. By using religion as the vehicle to distance and isolate myself from mainstream America, I was in fact exercising something very American—my freedom of religion.

My own religious education was not launched in Baghdad, Iraq, but in a small apartment in a college town in Pennsylvania, where I used to accompany my mother to weekly religious studies and learn about the Islamic virtues of humility and sacrifice. At the weekly sermons, I remember the men had the benefit of spacious accommodations, while we women were relegated to a more cramped space along with the equally frustrated children.

Many of the Muslims who had immigrated to the United States from countries with very diverse backgrounds had only a superficial, culturally motivated attachment to their faith, and in order to transcend the many cultural boundaries that divided us, we had to embrace the common religion that united us; and we had to do so by subscribing to a generic, one-size-fits-all interpretation of religion that left little room for dissent. We developed a collective identity that became strongly dependent on our ability to live out a romanticized vision of a community bound not so much by ideology as by conformity in religious practice.

I willingly embraced the values of social justice and tolerance that formed the underlying principles of my faith, and I did so by submitting, with strict adherence, to religious laws, rigid social norms, and a limited world view that would gratify my deepest longing for kinship and community. For example, I was taught that anything that attracts a man should be concealed, so logically—since anything, including my voice, can attract a man—I should not speak in mixed company. In addition, I was taught that I should not seek or wish to associate with non-Muslims, so I should give up my dearest friend, who was a devout Christian. As absurd as this may sound, the manifestation of that flawed logic became increasingly difficult to overlook, as more Muslims were beginning to indulge in this vision, not only in theory but in practice. And that was when the first seeds of doubt were planted; but, nonetheless, I clung to the all-or-nothing mentality which dictates that anything that has a proclivity toward corruption is harmful and should be avoided. And so beauty, art, music, and of course freedom, along with the politics that tolerated them, all had the potential of corrupting society, and so were at least implicitly renounced by my faith community. And while my mind was capable of accommodating my newly developing Islamic identity, my body rebelled by secretly entertaining the possibility that those very same things that have the potential to corrupt man, also have an even greater potential to elevate him. I held these subversive thoughts in secret.

So when my American government teacher asked me to identify myself as a Republican or Democrat, I proudly declared that I was a Muslim fundamentalist. And when my more liberal Arab classmates complained that in their hometown, young boys were being instructed to throw paint at women who walked with exposed legs, I tearfully spoke on behalf of those boys who I believed had the right to fight for the kind of moral society they wanted. And when I wrote my first article for a local newsletter at age eighteen, titled *Wake Up Muslim,* I paraphrased my entire new ideology in the last paragraph, where I wrote, "The infidel will not be our greatest challenge to the establishment of the Islamic State, it will be the moderate Muslim, the one who has become assimilated and finally put up his white picket fence and is excited about the prospect of voting for the first time. They will be our strongest critics as we make our way back to the path of God."

After graduating from college and in my first trimester of pregnancy with my son, I began a more formal religious education in the hopes of arming myself with the intellectual arguments that would lend credibility to the life I had chosen to lead. And so I left for a convention in Chicago and was greeted with a profound example of what happens when beliefs and dogma are taken to their logical conclusion. I spent three days in the company of women who were shrouded from head to toe—even their hands were gloved. A male scholar gave most of the lectures from behind a cloth screen and could only be observed live through a television set. But how could he have seen anyone, since I was one of the few who did not cover my face? But even that did not last, because one of the women protested against the necessity of seeing the man at all, arguing that we can hear the wisdom of his words without the distraction of his physical presence. I wondered if next we would have to read his words on a teleprompter lest we become titillated by his masculine voice. I was bewildered and confused and could no longer attribute the periodic vomiting spells I was having to just morning sickness. The seeds of dissent and doubt were planted, and my rebellious nature demanded some recourse.

In protest I entered the market area where women could only enter during specified hours. I walked around pretending to shop, knowing that at any moment I was going to be hauled off by one of the men, and sure enough, my protest lasted only five minutes. You would think that this experience would have sufficiently turned me off to this brand of religion altogether, but oh no, I resigned myself instead to study further, deciding that I had to get my act together in the interest of that heart which was now beating stronger than ever in my womb. And so I did just that, and persisted for another five years.

In spite of all the internal contradictions I harbored, it was of my own free will that I devoted myself to a code of beliefs and notions that had been passed on to me by the conservative religious wisdom of my community. And it was of my own free will that I committed myself, without reservation, to the noble profession of motherhood. But it was never my choice to bear what I initially perceived to be a grand cosmic misunderstanding. After investing my entire self in loving and sheltering my heart, my heart had, for reasons unknown, begun to rebel against me. The only way I knew to suppress this rebellion was to demand an answer to the one question which plagues every religious person when things go awry: *Why?!*

Why is my heart, in the form of my five-year-old son, not even willing to acknowledge me as his mother? For what crime was he or I being punished? Why, after I had honored my commitments with the tenacity of a good Muslim housewife, was I not reaping the reward of my love and loyalty? The objective and dispassionate answer to these questions, given by the many professionals who examined him, was that my son was suffering from a neurological disorder which affects the functioning of his brain, a disorder commonly known as autism. But that was the official explanation of a scientist, and certainly not the answer I was seeking.

Even my coreligionists and spiritual advisors could only resort to common clichés in their futile attempts to answer the unspoken question in my mind, by reminding me that all things happen for a reason, and that tribulations are just a test from God. But what they really meant is that all things should happen for a worthy reason, and that it was my task to formulate a noble explanation to lend credence to my suffering, and if I failed to do this, then I would have failed that divine test and with it the lost opportunity to become closer to God.

But I refused to give my life meaning by capitalizing on my son's anguish. I refused to be a willing victim, knowing that the temptation to play that role was only a selfish technique to alleviate my own pain. To find meaning through suffering was, to me, another form of sacrilegious idolization of my own identity. The reliance on anything, especially the opportunity of becoming a consecrated martyr, was a crutch that was more dangerous to me than all the crutches of worldly pleasures combined. And so I declined to take such a test, where the prospect of success in this world would, in my mind, be a failure in the next. I elected to fail this test of my saintliness, but not as a means to prove my commitment as a mother to her son, but rather to prove my faith and commitment to that which I loved even more than my son: my God Allah. The God who would not fail me, even if I failed myself. By doing nothing I had done something I believed was the greatest act of faith. I submitted myself to God with a kind of severity that sent me on autopilot, and I did this by clinging to the belief that if I idealized my faith even further, it would translate into the kind of divine intervention that would not only transform my son back to the healthy boy he'd been prior to his diagnosis, but would also transform me from a dogmatic monotheist, where there is only one God, to a mystic, where there is ONLY God. Only God and nothing else, not even the ego-bound desire for a healthy son.

My greatest challenge was to avoid the temptation to be a do-gooder, to become the stereotypical hyperactive, vigilant parent of a special needs child, someone who, as a result of this family crisis, all of a sudden finds God and confirms to herself and the world that bad things happen to good people for very good reasons. If I was going to suffer with integrity, then I must at least be honest and admit that my only ambition was to either cure my son, or cure myself by conquering all my desires, in the hope that all my sorrow would be supplanted by the divine light of a crutchless existence.

While for some, spiritual growth or decline is a process, for me it was an event that started with a private declaration to take trust in God to a whole new level. And so I adhered to everything, while believing in nothing, knowing that my unyielding belief system had become my single greatest worldly attachment. And so my journey began not with a visit to a religious guru or attendance at another religious convention, nor was it inspired by my little five-year-old emaciated autistic boy, who was only capable of living in the present moment; my journey began rather with a five-year-old girl who lived in the very distant past.

That girl was Helen Keller, a girl who had all the potential to be a human with intellect, but who was reduced to a state of near savagery because she only had one sense from which to learn— the sense of touch. She was unable to communicate until Anne Sullivan, also known as the "miracle worker," in a desperate effort to help her learn to communicate, removed her from the comfort of her family home and became her only source of survival. She required Helen to satisfy her own needs through the only means that Sullivan would allow—communication. In doing this Anne Sullivan transformed a wild child into an accomplished woman.

It was her story which compelled me, in an act of reasoned

faith, to attempt to do for my son what Anne Sullivan had done for Helen Keller. With the help of my dearest and oldest devout Christian friend, Amy, who awaited my arrival in Ohio, I was about to embark on what was supposed to be a three-month project but which actually lasted for over a year. I would have to rely on the kindness of strangers, including one minister, a gay couple, one atheist, and a couple of lost souls, all of them volunteering to facilitate the process to help cure my son through a diet of prayer and Anne-Sullivan-style behavior therapy. I would be forced to rely on a community of people who were a stark contrast to the only Muslim community I had ever really known. It was an experiment my friend Amy and I later dubbed "boot camp."

So I packed a few rudimentary items and, strapping my son in a car, left my family behind, including my two other children, the youngest of which I had to wean from my breast, to set out across the country toward Ohio to join Amy, who was a remarkably gifted teacher, as we endeavored to become modern-day Anne Sullivans.

When I left my home state of Kansas, my son was still in diapers and could only venture out in a stroller. Nothing took more priority than finding some way of silencing his endless bloodcurdling screams, the cries that were his only means of communication. I went with the determination to adhere more faithfully than I ever had to my religion, including its every injunction and prescription, while remaining strictly vacant of any ideas which might interfere with the divine guidance I so desperately needed. I went clad in black from head to toe, wearing my Islamic dress with a kind of austerity which made me the object of many stares, directed both at my dress and at the son who appeared normal but who threw violent tantrums that left everyone wondering whether he was being abused at the hands of this stern-looking Muslim mother. I left armed with a short to-do list of only two items. First, cure my son at any cost. And second, find a recipe to ensure that my union with God remained a choice, not something forced on me by these circumstances. My greatest desire, to be close to God, had become my greatest fear, not because I did not yearn for closeness but because I never wanted faith to be the product of circumstance instead of choice. I did not want salvation as a mercy, but only as something I had rightfully earned.

I held on to the defective notion that if I could annihilate my ego, maybe by some divine law, God would give my son the ego he lacked. All the things in our nature that we deem as vices, like jealousy, pride, arrogance, vanity, and even desire, are the very things which some autistics lack. My son's senses were incapable of processing information from his environment, and without sensory input, there can be no concepts and therefore no language. Without this ability there could not be any religion. Without a system of specific neurons called "mirror neurons," which were most likely damaged in my son's brain, rituals, religion, and culture could not have been transmitted over the ages. It never dawned on me that the thing I was trying to eradicate in myself— my ego, the part of us which is attached to the past and the present and to the abstract ideas of self and "theory of mind"—was the very thing which would have cured my son. How is it that something which was spiritually destructive for me could be so good for him?

The answer to that unasked question came the night I stopped at the motel on my way to the holy land of Ohio, where my son spoke to me for the first time in his short life. But he did not speak to me using words, rather with the sound of silence. A silent moment for my screaming, wailing son was a clearly transmitted spoken word.

My son was a mystic. But unlike a mystic who can snap out of his ecstatic unitary state of timelessness, my son could not. He was stuck in a perpetual state of oblivion, always in the present moment, where any change in his environment, no matter how inconsequential, was perceived as an assault on his senses. And just like a mystic, he would be happy if left to his own devices to numb himself with repetitive behaviors and drown out the world. He was the physical manifestation of a mystic caught in an ecstatic state so intense that he could not even sense his own physical being, not knowing where his body ended and the world began. Seeing this made me realize that an ego was indispensable to our spiritual evolution, for how could we ever gaze at the beatific vision if we did not have ego-bound eyes with which to see and interpret what we saw, eyes that were constrained by an identity, a self that is separate from that vision. Without it we would be like a saltwater fish in search of the very ocean we occupy, an ocean we can only recognize if we had the capacity to think abstractly and conceptually. And for my son, as is the case for all of humankind, the only way to think abstractly or to think at all, is to evolve the breathing mechanism of an independent ego.

When we arrived at the motel room I laid him on the edge of the bed, only to have him hurl himself at me and sucker-punch me right in the face. I forced a bit of food in his mouth only to have him spit it at me. We fought it out all night, and I knew that if he succeeded in conquering me, in conquering my ego—that if I allowed him to cut me down until I had no desire left—we would have become one and the same, both of us stripped of our desire to live. And if the choice had to be made, it was going to be made in the interest of life—a life with all its desires and pleasures and an ego that was strong enough for the two of us.

My son, like that metaphorical fish, could only find solace when immersed in a pool of water. The warmth of that water calmed him, took him back to his state of primordial unconsciousness by numbing his senses. But I had no water to relieve him. I hadn't slept in days, managing to stay awake on a diet of caffeine and sugar; he had not slept or eaten a real meal for days, either. And in spite of his obvious exhaustion he was still fighting me with everything he had, not wanting to eat or sleep, but screaming as if he had just awoken from a horrifying nightmare.

All I could do was leave him to bounce off the walls and plead, with his cries, for help. So I set out to help him in the only way I knew how. I laid out a towel to serve as a prayer mat and stripped off my dirty clothes, letting him whimper in the corner of the room; I'd grown accustomed to drowning out his weeping. I was able to focus as I faced Mecca as precisely as my compass would guide me and, standing as straight as my legs could hold me, began to make my ritual prayers. I tried the best I could to comply with the strictest directives for prayer, making my ablutions twice, then a third time just to make certain that every prescribed limb had been washed thoroughly. I made my prostrations in perfect form. And when I did not feel that I had made my prayers with truthful intentions, I repeated my prayer again, then again. I found myself doubting that I had fully completed my prayers without mistake, and so I continued to pray, attempting to make each prayer more perfect than the one before. And after every prayer I made supplications.

But I found that my raised, open-palmed hands would continually turn into fists. Rather than extending my arms toward heaven, I was shaking my fists up at heaven, only to feel regret and start again. I made it my intention to supplicate politely and in a more rehearsed fashion. But the irony was that I did not feel the majesty of God in my polite supplications. I could only feel God in my rage, when my fists were clenched, when I was imploring and petitioning Him with a vengeance. And I could not explain why it was that when I prayed with shaking fists I felt like I was having an interaction with God, but when I prayed properly, I felt like I was having an interaction with my ego. An ego which reminded me to stay on the straight path of polite, submissive compliance. An ego which kept reminding me that my prayers would not be counted if I fell short on form or function. The ego which continually reminded me that I was a good girl. So with greater confusion and even more desperation, I got up again, determined to have a prayer that was both polite and compliant and that adhered to the highest standards of form as well as the greatest intentions of purity. By now my son was screaming louder than ever.

I had always been taught to approach prayer with the mindset that it may be the very last prayer I make, and therefore the last opportunity to repent and redeem myself. And remembering this I stood there with a sense of great despair, knowing that it was highly likely that this could be my very last prayer, for I had reached the end of myself. If I failed in making it, my faith would crumble against my own will. I started to stand, but I was so overwrought with grief that I just decided to supplicate first, and so I fell to my knees and started to negotiate on behalf of my soul. Dear God, I was prepared to give up every worldly accretion. There was nothing I would not do for you. I was not negotiating for my son's cure, what I wanted was something much simpler. I wanted a sign, a feeling, a deconstruction of doubt and faith in exchange for one ounce of knowledge. If I could just have one inkling of certainty that my pain was not in vain, then I would know that I could survive an entire world of screaming boys. But I felt nothing but despair. I was perhaps too vain, so I vowed that come tomorrow, I would not only cover my hair and my body, but my face as well. I negotiated until I had given up everything, my vanity, my marriage, my every desire, my every worldly possession. I gave up everything on that prayer mat, to no avail. No peace of mind would enter my heart.

Just as I was about to rebel, just as my hands were turning into fists, and my faith was about to descend into a permanent hatred, I faced down on the floor and tearfully swore that I would give up everything but my soul, I would even give up my son. And just as this thought entered my mind, my son became quiet and in his silence he made me realize that I was being untruthful. As I looked at him sitting peacefully for that one moment on the edge of the hotel bed with nothing but a diaper, I realized that I would sell my soul a million times over to give him but one night of blissful sleep.

But what I had initially interpreted as a sign encouraging me to compromise my soul in the interest of my heart, was really a sign to listen to a united heart and soul. To listen to the soul that knows no bounds except the ones that I have allowed others to set for it. Without faith or doubt, or even a shred of knowledge, I had the most glorious epiphany that has ever descended upon me, and just as I was about to praise God for the permission to do that, my son began to cry again. And without a second thought I jolted up, cast off my prayer clothes, and stepped outside carrying my son, wearing nothing but a cotton slip, armed only with a washcloth with which to muffle his cries. I ran down several flights of stairs, oblivious of my nakedness, looking for water, searching for water, looking for our *zamzam* water.

When I reached the lobby I stepped out into the hallway and tiptoed to the courtyard in the middle of the motel, my son clawing at me like a kitten all the while, the towel clenched between his jaws. I tiptoed down the carpeted corridor to the indoor courtyard where there was a large swimming pool lit only by the gigantic skylight spanning the ceiling directly above. It was the middle of the night and the pool was gated and closed by a decorative white picket fence. I could not break in the pool door, so with my son still clinging to me, his nails digging deep into my arms, I peeled him off of me, threw him over the fence, and standing up on a concrete ledge which held piles of towels, I swiftly leapt in after him. I grabbed him off the ground and slowly walked into the pool with his legs and arms wrapped tightly around me. As I glided around the pool his whimpers subsided and he began to relax, laying his shoulder on me for the first time in a long time. I was so tired that the prospect of falling asleep in the warm pool seemed dangerously inviting. I became completely unmindful of my state of undress and my bruises, and unafraid of the great probability that I would be caught.

I was happier than I had ever been, happy for the profound realization from my womb—the realization that happiness does not lie in knowing what path you are going to take, but in knowing that once you do find it you will have enough faith and courage in yourself to take it. And I knew that moment that I had the courage and the divine consent to do anything my heart desired.

I thanked God for the gifts of my womb that were the source of my wisdom, and for the realization that every time I, in an act of faith, followed a direction that was of my own mind and not an exercise in compliance, I was replacing my communal ego with a personal ego bound only by the sacred exchanges between my Lord and me.

To experience the sacred using my own senses, trusting in my own perception, is preferable to experiencing it through the watered-down perceptions of an entire community. It is also preferable to experiencing it through the perceptions of a mystic who takes comfort in being reminded of what and where we came from, but who never exits his ecstatic state fully understanding why we are here.

And why we are here, I believe, can be answered by looking at the human exception of my mystic son, who lacks the one faculty that most of us take for granted as a curse, but which is the greatest blessing bestowed upon us: our consciousness and our free will. To answer why is to recognize that every time we genuinely exercise our conscious free will by making judgments that transcend the prescriptions of others, we develop wings that allow us to fly away from the comfortable nest of safety and security, and to embark into the unknown, armed with the paradoxical realization that the further away we fly using our own wings, the closer we get to God. Flying is the answer to the question *why*. As Helen Keller once wrote, "One can never consent to creep when one feels an impulse to soar."

Why has my heart rebelled against me? I ask myself again, only this time the answer comes loud and clear: because I had consented to creep when I have always had the impulse to soar. My son may never develop the impulse or capacity to fly, but he has a much nobler calling than that. His calling is to remind us that he does not want to live in a world where others choose to creep as a mercy to him and in pity for the helpless and meek. If we do that, then all their suffering will have been in vain. He is here to remind us to claim the awesome responsibility of our own free will, and choose life, growth, and freedom.

As my son lay peacefully on my shoulder I thanked God for the capacity to think beyond the moment, but also to live within it. And so I lived within that timeless moment, imagining that I had my son back to the way he was only a few years earlier, to the way he used to be when he was a happy two-year-old who knew and loved his mother. And I thanked God for giving me the courage to enjoy that moment and every other moment from then on. I thanked God for the permission to make my own decisions without the sanction of some official religious authority. I thanked God for the realization that everything I had ever wanted and asked for was encapsulated in that which I prostrated to Him every time I prayed—my mind—and I thanked Him not only for the permission, but for the command to use it.

I thanked God for all the epiphanies that night, which ended when the sunrise broke through the skylight above and I heard the sound of movement as people began to wake up. Soaking wet, I climbed out of the pool, and too tired to climb up a single flight of stairs, I took the elevator, not caring who saw me. When I got to my room, I pulled back the covers on the bed and laid my son down to enjoy the remainder of his blissful sleep. And then standing in the middle of the room, still wet with the concentrated smell of chlorine in my hair, facing neither Mecca nor Minnesota, but knowing as surely as I knew I was standing there that I was facing God, I prepared to pray—not as if this was my last prayer, but as if it was my very first genuine prayer ever. And raising my hands toward heaven, my voice whispered and my heart exclaimed, *Allahu Akbar,* God is greater, God is greater, God is greater!

Years later, I know that the exterior manifestation of my life will never represent the more noble internal motivations of my heart. So outwardly I no longer wear my Islamic dress either religiously or as a means to express my Islamic identity, because I know who I am even if others don't. And although I have, by at least some of my coreligionists, been officially condemned to hell (as opposed to my former only *potentially* hell-bound status), I have never felt closer to heaven. In contrast to that first radical publication which I titled *Wake Up Muslim,* I now write for an e-zine with a progressive mission statement and, incidentally, the exact opposite title of *Muslim Wake Up.* In addition, on behalf of myself and of my son, who now knows and loves me, I have traded in my fundamentalist politics and voted for the first time. I am finally, religiously, politically, and officially declaring myself—an independent! As for my white picket fence, it, like my newly developing community of Muslims and non-Muslims, is still under construction.

MY SISTER'S PRAYER

Suheir Hammad

She has never heard a woman call her
To prayer   still she answers
Bears witness   five times a day
She faces East
And washes her body   covers her human form
In preparation to meet the Most High

She raises her hands
Aware of all who have come before her
Folds hands on her breast
Right on top of left
Between Arabic words   heart beat   breath
She raises her hands
In hope of all that will follow

Humble and knowing she needs no defense
She bows
Before no man
She bows
Behind the men
She bows
Knowing angels will raise her back up

She prays on rugs   carpets   cardboard   earth
She prays hungry   ill   misguided   hurt

All the while calling on Perfection Grace

Head to the ground
Even the floor she walks upon becomes sacred
She prays in prescribed form but knows
There is no language the Universe does not accept
There is no posture void of God

She is Sarah's daughter
She is Hagar's daughter
And like her father Abraham her tent is open
In the four directions
For each wind will carry her prayers
From each direction will come her blessings
From the trees and the rocks
From the seas and the hills

She sits alone knowing she is one of many
She sits alone knowing no one can petition for her

All the while calling on Compassion   Mercy

Her hands are open
Her father taught her to read the words
Her mothers teach her to live them
Her brothers told her to live by the law
Her sisters tell her the only law is Love

She invokes peace over her right shoulder
Then her left
She sits alone with all that daily creates her
She sits alone and patiently waits
To experience the feminine force of the Divine
Within her own body   her own face

ACKNOWLEDGMENTS

Thank you to Tara Roberts, who saw this book before I did, planted the seed, and watered it regularly. Many thanks to Asra Nomani and Samina Ali, who provided feedback greatly and unselfishly. Thanks to Gayatri Patnaik, wisely named for the wealthy goddess of knowledge who rests on a lotus and has a view of the whole world, for her patience and professionalism and belief in this project. With gratitude and love, thank you Nichelle Holder, Khabira Abdul-Faattah, and Shanè and Stefon Harris, because you loved me unconditionally before I did. And thank you Umi, Abu, and Mahmood, who've always related to me as the greatest possibility.

Saleemah Abdul-Ghafur

helped to establish *Azizah* magazine, the first lifestyle magazine for Muslim women in North America. She is on the board of the Progressive Muslim Union and is affiliated with Atlanta Habitat for Humanity and the Atlanta Women's Foundation. Saleemah is committed to a life of service and presents frequently on popular culture, Islam, and women. She lives in Atlanta, Georgia.

Su'ad Abdul-Khabeer

is a poet committed to personal and popular upliftment. A native of Brooklyn, New York, she has lived and traveled throughout the United States, the Middle East, Africa, and Europe. She is currently pursuing her Ph.D. in cultural anthropology at Princeton University.

Sham-e-Ali al-Jamil

is a South Asian poet and writer, whose work has appeared in *SALT Journal, Roots & Culture,* and *Mizna.* She is also a lawyer who has worked on the welfare rights of survivors of intimate-partner violence.

Samina Ali

is the author of *Madras on Rainy Days*. She is the recipient of the Rona Jaffe Foundation award for fiction and has written for such publications as *Self, Child,* the *New York Times,* and the *San Francisco Chronicle*. She lives in California with her son.

Sarah Eltantawi

is a frequent media commentator on American Muslim affairs and Middle East policy, and has written on counterterrorism for *Upfront,* the *New York Times* magazine for teens. Sarah is a cofounder of the Progressive Muslim Union of North America and she is pursuing her Ph.D. in religious studies at Harvard University.

Yousra Y. Fazili

has written about sexuality and Islamic law for the *Encyclopedia of Women in Islamic Cultures* and the *American Journal of Islamic Social Sciences*. Ms. Fazili graduated from Brown University in 1999. She traveled to Egypt as a Fulbright Scholar, where she studied Arabic and researched Islamic law and modernization at Al-Azhar University. She received her J.D. from American University, Washington College of Law, and currently works as an attorney. She lives in New York.

Suheir Hammad

was born in Amman, Jordan, to Palestinian refugee parents and grew up in the United States. She is an active poet and performer. Her work has appeared in award-winning anthologies and in various journals. Suheir was an original writer of and performer in the Tony Award–winning *Def Poetry Jam* on Broadway. Her recent book of poems is *Zaatar Diva*. She lives in New York City.

Mohja Kahf's

first poetry book is *Emails from Scheherazad.* Her book *Western Representations of the Muslim Woman* examines gender and Islam in early Western literatures. Kahf's first novel, a fictional account of growing up in a Klan-beleaguered Muslim community in the Midwest, is due from Carroll & Graf in 2005. She writes an Islamically grounded column on sexuality for the progressive Muslim website, www.MuslimWakeUp.com. Dr. Kahf, who grew up happily eating unripe apples on the ISNA farm in Indiana, is an associate professor of comparative literature at the University of Arkansas in Fayetteville, where she lives with her husband and three children.

Precious Rasheeda Muhammad,

an author, lecturer, publisher, and researcher on the growth and development of Islam in America and the Muslim American experience, discovered a Muslim ex-slave narrative, founded an educational publishing company (www.islaminamerica.com), and is a graduate of Harvard Divinity School. She lives in Cambridge, Massachusetts, with her husband, Carl.

Asra Q. Nomani

is a former staff reporter for the *Wall Street Journal* and has written about politics, business, popular culture, sexuality, and Islam. She is the author of *Tantrika* and *Standing Alone in Mecca,* about reclaiming the rightful place of women in Islam. She has also written for *Salon,* the *Washington Post,* the *New York Times, Cosmopolitan,* and *Sports Illustrated for Women.* A native of India, Ms. Nomani lives in Morgantown, West Virginia, with her son.

Manal Omar

is currently the country director for Women for Women International – Iraq. She is responsible for establishing the local chapter office for Iraq and has been working out of Baghdad since July 2003. Previously, Manal worked with the World Bank and the Global Development Network. She currently splits her time between Iraq and Jordan.

Aroosha Zoq Rana

is an entrepreneur, educator, writer, performer, collective builder, and sister in the struggle for social change. She has traveled and worked in Colombia, the Dominican Republic, Pakistan, Boston, New York, and Washington, D.C. In each community she builds connections with people across culture, creed, language, and gender barriers, finding musical performance to be the most effective and personally motivating vehicle to do just that.

Khalida Saed

is an American Muslim lesbian and uses a pseudonym for safety reasons. She speaks and writes about faith, sexuality, and gender and has been working with Al-Fatiha Foundation since 2001.

Asia Sharif-Clark

is president and CEO of the Sharif-Clark Group, LLC, an Internet-based consulting company for parents of young children. She has twelve years of combined classroom and community teaching experience, including English as a Second Language. Asia received her Master of Arts in pre-elementary education in 1999. She lives in Suffolk, Virginia, with her husband, James, and their sons, Tariq and Rashad.

Khadijah Sharif-Drinkard

is vice president, senior counsel for MTV Networks, where she specializes in entertainment law. She has committed herself to giving back through the use of one-on-one mentoring as well as conducting self-empowerment seminars. While Khadijah has spent the greater part of her life serving as a motivational speaker here in the United States, she has taken her message of activism around the world. She served on New York City mayor David N. Dinkins's delegation to South Africa, was selected from a pool of scholars from across the nation to be a youth ambassador to Russia, and represented Muslim American women at the United Nations Fourth World Conference on Women in Beijing, China. She has been featured as a young political activist on several television programs and has been spotlighted in the *New York Times*. She lives with her husband and daughter in Maplewood, New Jersey.

Inas Younis

was born in Mosul, Iraq, and migrated with her family to the United States at the age of eight. She is a freelance writer and is now beginning work on her first novel, titled *Monads*. She resides in the Kansas City area with her husband and three children.